BERBER VILLAGE

BERBER VILLAGE

*The Story of the Oxford University Expedition
to the High Atlas Mountains of Morocco*

BY

BRYAN CLARKE

THE TRAVEL BOOK CLUB
121 CHARING CROSS ROAD
LONDON W.C.2.

Printed in Great Britain by
Latimer, Trend & Co. Ltd., Plymouth

To
G. M. C.
with love

Contents

Explanation		xiv
1.	Night on an African Road	1
2.	Plans and Preparations	5
3.	'Tartarin' Moves	17
4.	El Moghreb el Aksa	25
5.	Red City, White Castle	38
6.	The Valley of the Ait Rbaa	65
7.	Pillars of the Sky	84
8.	Alarms and Excursions	103
9.	Never to Dream	118
10.	The Encroaching Desert	127
11.	'Tartarin' Moves Again	145
	Epilogue	150
	Appendix with Acknowledgments	153

MAP   PAGE

The High Atlas Mountains   xvi

Acknowledgments

We are indebted to the following for permission to quote copyright material:

Messrs. Jonathan Cape Ltd. for lines quoted from 'A Ticket for the Reading Room' from *The Dorking Thigh* by William Plomer; Mr. Robert Frost; Messrs. Henry Holt & Co. Inc. New York and Messrs. Jonathan Cape Ltd. for lines quoted from 'Neither Out Far Nor in Deep' and 'Desert Places' from *The Complete Poems of Robert Frost*.

Explanation

THIS is the story of a journey to Morocco in the summer of 1955. We called it an Expedition, but only in the sense of its being a body of men setting out for a distant place. We went to study the life, human and otherwise, of valleys in the Moroccan Atlas. Little scientific work had been done there, but the region had previously been visited by several European travellers, and had been mapped by the French. We were not exploring.

We visited the country at a time of political disturbance, and had every reason to expect that the Administration would be preoccupied and inclined to disregard or discourage visitors. We were thus particularly grateful to both the French and Moroccan authorities for their most generous and friendly co-operation. I am sure that we could not have completed, or even started, our work without the assistance of the many officials and others with whom we made contact. Detailed acknowledgments of the people and organizations who so kindly helped us are given in the Appendix.

It would have been impossible to write an honest account of our journey without mentioning the vexed subject of politics. None of us were experts. We went to Morocco with little or no knowledge of the political situation, and our opinions grew from our own rather limited experiences. I have voiced these opinions because they played so large a part in our lives, but they must not be taken too seriously. We spoke neither Berber nor Arabic, and all our conversations were through an interpreter. In some ways, however, we had a unique opportunity to hear the views of both sides. The majority of writers to visit the country have travelled either directly under the auspices of the French, or with the assistance of the Nationalist parties. They have often had a political axe to grind. So perhaps our observations, naïve though they may be, will have some value.

When, from time to time, I have criticized the French or the Moroccans, I hope the reader will understand that it has been done with a full knowledge and appreciation of the good in both, and with a profound sense of gratitude for the help they have given us.

A story of this sort must to some extent be fiction. I have described only the more exciting happenings of our trip, and must inevitably have given an over-coloured picture of the Moroccan scene. Memory and imagination, too, are at fault. We kept diaries, but none of them are complete, and there are many incidents about whose interpretation we differ. I am tempted to echo the words of Washington Irving in his *Tales of a Traveller*: 'I am always at a loss to know how much to believe of my own stories.'

I have had some difficulty in spelling Arabic names; the possible English transliterations are innumerable. The reader has only to look at five books on Islam, and he will find as many spellings of Mohammed (or Muhammed or Mahomet). The same applies to almost any other Arabic word. In Morocco the situation is complicated because some of the place-names and titles have an anglicized spelling (e.g. *Marrakesh* or *Pasha*) distinct from the French (*Marrakech* or *Pacha*). In fact, the inhabitants of Marrakesh pronounce it *Mraksh*. I have given up all attempts to be consistent, since in every case it will be perfectly clear to which town or official I am referring.

Many people helped us with the expedition, but there are also a number who have specifically assisted the writing of this book. I would like to thank especially the other members of the party, in particular Colin Pennycuick, who has allowed me to use his diaries, and Humphrey Beckett, for letting me plagiarize his descriptions of several activities in which I did not take part. I am grateful also to the many friends who have read and criticized the manuscript. Ann Jewkes, John Currey, and Hugh Wallace deserve special thanks.

The faults, inaccuracies, and half-truths are, alas, my own.

B.C.

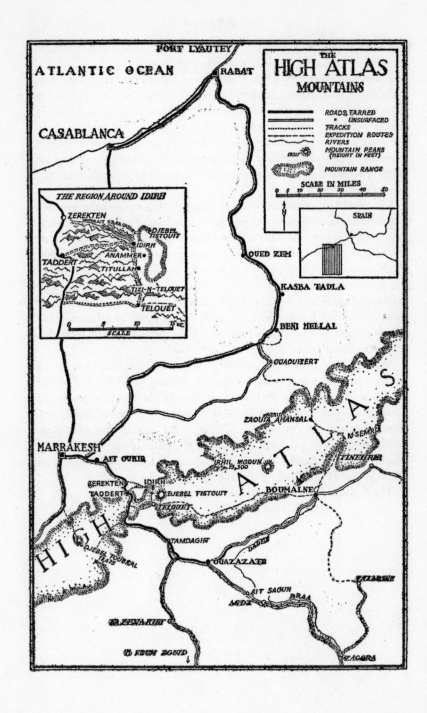

THE
HIGH ATLAS
MOUNTAINS

ROADS, TARRED
" UNSURFACED
TRACKS
EXPEDITION ROUTES
RIVERS
MOUNTAIN PEAKS
(HEIGHT IN FEET)
MOUNTAIN RANGE

SCALE IN MILES
0 5 10 20 30 40 50

N

SPAIN

ATLANTIC OCEAN

PORT LYAUTEY

RABAT

CASABLANCA

OUED ZEM

KASBA TADLA

BENI MELLAL

OUAOUIZERT

THE REGION AROUND IDIRH

ZEREKTEN
TIZI RBAA
DJEBEL TISTOUIT
IDIRH
ANAMMER
TADDERT
TITULLAH
TIZI-N-TELOUET
TELOUET

SCALE
0   5   10   15 km

ZAOUIA AHANSAL

M'SEMRIR

MARRAKESH

AIT OURIR

IRHIL MGOUN
13,300

TINERHIR

ZEREKTEN
IDIRH
TADDERT
DJEBEL TISTOUIT
TELOUET

A T L A S

BOUMALNE

H I G H

DJEBEL TOUBKAL
13,675

TAMDAGHT

DADES

OUAZAZATE

TAZZARINE

AIT SAOUN
AGDZ
DRAA

TIZI-N-TEST

TIZI-N-TICHKA

ZAGORA

CHAPTER ONE

Night on an African Road

TEN minutes passed before the first car came.

I held up my hand, and stepped out into the glare of the approaching headlights. The car seemed to slow, while the driver hesitated, but suddenly it accelerated straight towards me. I jumped clear and it swept by, sounding its horn, to disappear into the darkness. The second, third, and fourth cars did not even slacken speed.

At the frontier that morning the customs officer had warned us:

'It is best to drive only during the day. But if you *must* travel at night, take care. If anyone tries to hail you on the road, don't stop. There have been quite a few ambushes recently. They pretend to be motorists in distress. But if you try to help them. . . .' He had left the sentence unfinished.

We did not know the country, and we took the warning seriously, determining to reach Port Lyautey before nightfall. But we did not consider the possibility that we ourselves might break down, and that other motorists might have been similarly warned. The thought of five undergraduates of Oxford staging an ambush on a Moroccan road was an amusing one. Perhaps the dust of travel had made us appear more villainous than usual. Whatever the cause, the effect was clear. Not a car would stop.

After a long time, a convoy of vehicles approached from the south. I waved them down, without much hope of success. But there was a screech of brakes, a flashing of lights, and they came to a halt. I noticed two motor-cycles among them, and from one of these a uniformed figure dismounted. He approached cautiously, waving a sub-machine-gun, and shouting above the roar of the engines.

'Who are you? What do you want?'

'English. We've had a breakdown and wanted to get to Port Lyautey for help.'

'But we're going north!' He was irritable, but he looked relieved.

'None of the cars going south would stop.'

B   I

'I am sorry. It is the ambushes. You crossed the border this morning?'
I nodded.

'You haven't chosen a good time. Nevertheless, welcome to
Morocco. I will stop the next one for you.'

The 'next one' was an ambulance. The driver looked out anxiously
at the collection of cars, motor-cycles and policemen.

'Trouble?' he asked.

'No. These English have had a breakdown. You must take them to
Port Lyautey.'

'Can't take all of them. We've got a couple of *indigènes* in the back.'

'Take two. They can bring help if the others don't follow.'

The ambulance driver and his companions climbed out to open the
doors. The two wounded Moroccans, who lay on low stretchers, were
pushed groaning to one side. Humphrey and I were sandwiched in, the
doors slammed, and we were soon speeding towards the town.

The driving was inspired, but the passengers did not appreciate it.
As we swerved and bumped on the road, the two wounded men cried
out in pain. One of them, tossing on his stretcher, clutched at my foot.
It seemed to give him some comfort, for he gripped it firmly until the
end of the journey.

When the suburbs of the city came into view, the driver relaxed
over the wheel and lit a cigarette. His companion, who had been
silently nursing a sub-machine-gun, whistled softly to himself and
stowed it away under the seat. We stopped in the main street. It was a
relief to get out into the cool night air, away from the sickly sweet
smell of blood.

Although it was not yet nine o'clock, Port Lyautey was completely
deserted. There was not even a policeman to be seen. We searched for
a telephone, but without success. Finally, in desperation, I banged on
the door of a shuttered café. There was no reply. I banged again, and
the noise echoed loud across the empty street. Then bolts were drawn
back, the door opened an inch and an eye surveyed us from the darkness
beyond.

'What do you want?'

'I am sorry to disturb you, but I wondered if we could use your
telephone.'

The door opened a little more to reveal a French woman of middle
age, draped in the shapeless black uniform of her kind.

'Of course. I am sorry to appear suspicious, but one has to be so careful these days. Particularly tonight. There were bombs in Casablanca this morning and whenever there is trouble in "Casa", there is trouble here. It is a strain. But you, of course, will understand. The English have the same sort of trouble in Kenya. Here, it is just like Kenya.'

Madame was obviously delighted to have someone to talk to. She kept up an animated conversation throughout the telephone call, and continued until we were once more outside her door.

We made our way through deserted streets to the Place de la République, where we had arranged to meet the others. Humphrey went off to search for a garage, while I waited in the little garden which occupied the centre of the square. The white modern buildings shone in the moonlight. I thought about the people within them, wondering if they were frightened. Perhaps they felt safe behind their shuttered windows.

Humphrey soon returned to interrupt my imaginings, and we walked together round the square, finding at the far end a 'Bar Americain' which was still open. Inside, beneath shaded lights, a pretty girl was polishing glasses. A solitary customer, perched on a high stool, gazed gloomily into space. He was, appropriately, an American. But he was not inclined to conversation. He bade us good evening, commented unprintably upon the desolation of life, and then returned to contemplating his empty glass. The girl smiled, and served us Dubonnets with ice. But she too was silent.

Ten minutes later our truck turned into the square, the others safely aboard. Peter had managed to repair it soon after Humphrey and I had left in the ambulance. There remained only to find somewhere to sleep. After a brief search we discovered a convenient plot of waste ground. At one end of it a gang of men was noisily pulling down a big tent; at the other, there was a heterogeneous collection of caravans and lorries. We parked near them and set up our Primuses for supper. An aromatic stew was soon bubbling in the pot.

Perhaps it was this that attracted our visitor. He strolled over from a nearby caravan to inquire who we were, and what we were about. Having been satisfied, he told us of himself. He was an acrobat, performing in the circus which was being so busily dismantled. It came each summer from Corsica to tour the larger Moroccan towns. Usually it was a success, but this year had been disastrous.

'On our first night in Port Lyautey—that was the night before last—

we had a full house. Then there were the *événements* in Casa. Tonight, fifteen people turned up. Fifteen people! It has been the same in the other towns, Petitjean, Meknés, Fez. We can't live on audiences like that. We are going home.'

We consoled him with stew, and he went his way.

When supper was done, and the dishes washed, we climbed wearily into our sleeping bags. I lay on my back, listening to the noises of camels which were tethered nearby, and watching the bright stars. They were the same stars, the same constellations. There were people in England, no doubt, watching them as I did. People who were not afraid of a knock on the door or a breakdown on the road. People who would never know of life in a country divided within itself.

I remembered that an Arab on a donkey had passed us when we were stopped by the roadside. We saw him first as a speck on the deserted horizon. Half an hour later he rode by, his long face impassive in the dusk. He did not greet us. His expression did not show sympathy or dislike, only lack of interest. The gulf between us, at that moment, seemed enormous. Could we ever understand them, or they us? Were we not expecting too much, in planning to live with them in their villages?

The answers came in due course, and some of them were surprising.

CHAPTER TWO

Plans and Preparations

Unaware of other people,
Peace and war and politics,
Down the pavement see him totter
Following his *idée fixe*.

WILLIAM PLOMER

I THINK it was Stephen Leacock who first compared the system of teaching at Oxford to the preparation of kippers. Each week the undergraduate is obliged to write an essay on a chosen subject. At the tutorial he reads it. His tutor listens, says nothing and smokes. Three or four years of curing in an atmosphere of tobacco produce, by some mysterious alchemy, an educated man.

My own tutor was unconventional. Believing perhaps that the curing process should be internal rather than external, he specialized in boiled sweets, and at the beginning of each tutorial he would offer two or three to his unfortunate pupil. There was method in his generosity, for it rendered the ensuing essay almost completely inaudible.

One week in the spring of 1954, however, even the rattling confections failed to conceal the inadequacy of my work. It was a very bad essay indeed. When I had stumbled through it, my tutor—a considerate man—politely changed the subject.

'What', he asked, 'are you going to do in the summer vacation?'

I had no idea, but I appreciated the diversion. Anything was better than discussing the essay, so I mentioned Morocco. I mentioned it because a visit there had long been one of my ambitions. I cannot give any respectable reason, but the idea started when I was being trained as a pilot in the Canadian Middle West.

Someone has observed that many of the world's philosophies have been evolved in the desert; there is little else to do. Manitoba is not exactly a desert, but it is flat, with a great deal of wheat. It was very productive of ideas.

5

This one happened to stick. A friend and I determined to visit Fez. The name was connected in our minds with 'Romance' and 'The Mysterious East'. It became a sort of watchword. We hailed each other with it, and it inspired us, for some reason, to spend a week-end camping in the north, where the wheatlands give way to equally monotonous stretches of virgin bush. The excursion was not a success, because we were forced to retreat, after a single night, from the enormous swarms of mosquitoes. (Large animals are scarce in northern Manitoba, and human beings almost unknown. The mosquitoes go a long time between meals.)

My tutor was interested in Morocco. A study of some of its animals, he said, would be very instructive, and little work had been done.

Scientists believe that in remote ages, when sheets of ice crept down to cover most of Europe, many European animal groups were gradually forced south into Spain and Morocco. Here they found an equable climate and an abundance of food. But as the ice retreated the Moroccan plains became hotter and hotter. Some animal populations escaped upwards to the cooler mountains, and have been isolated there ever since. It would be rewarding to find out the effects of this long period of isolation, during which the populations must have changed and become adapted to the conditions of their new home. It was reasonable to expect that some of them would have changed enough to be classified as species new to science. Furthermore, Morocco supports many animals characteristic of the African continent, and these might well have interbred with European immigrants to form hybrid groups. A study of such hybrids would throw further light on the way in which animal species have evolved.

My tutor's enthusiasm was contagious, I went away determined to collect those animals.

A few days later I heard of the Oxford University Exploration Club. Its function is to assist its members to go on expeditions, and it has access to certain funds which help to finance them. My informant was a member, and offered to take me along to a meeting.

It was a chastening experience. The wide oak-panelled college room seemed to be full of large, bronzed, efficient men. Fragments of conversation drifted across to me.

'. . . a devil of a lot of trouble with the long sled—kept freezing up . . .', '. . . hanging on the South face . . . couldn't go up or down.'
'. . . So they fitted an outboard on to the dugout and it went like a

dream . . .', '. . . and then the bear just turned round and ambled off. . . .'

I sat in a corner, feeling very small. Somebody came up and asked me where I had been the previous summer. I said, 'Normandy,' and he wandered away, looking faintly embarrassed. Eventually I could stand it no longer. I cornered an unfortunate victim, and told him highly exaggerated tales of the rigours of winter in northern Manitoba. I later discovered that he was the leader of an expedition to the Arctic.

I became a member of the Exploration Club and attended the meetings—hoping that somebody would invite me to join an expedition. No one did. It was clear that I would have to organize one myself.

The funds to which the club has access are not great, and the demand far exceeds the supply. Thus it is that many expeditions are conceived but few are born. An 'Expedition Council', largely composed of senior members of the university, meets every spring to consider the numerous proposals, and to select two or three which they will support. Their task is not an easy one, for they are presented with many grandiloquent schemes, promising tremendous achievements at negligible cost, and in order to separate the practicable from the impracticable they demand very detailed plans and estimates.

Having decided that I must prepare such a plan, I was uncertain what to do next. So I started to write letters. I wrote to anyone who might conceivably know something about the country. I wrote to the French Tourist Office, to travel agents, to University Departments. I pestered the authors of books on Morocco. Knowing that he had recently visited Marrakesh, I even wrote to Sir Winston Churchill. This piece of impertinence elicited a very polite and forbearing reply from one of his secretaries. The envelope was marked, '10 Downing Street' and, in heavy type 'PRIME MINISTER'. It rested for some days in the college letter-rack, and created a mild sensation among my friends.

As the replies came in to this first rash of correspondence, I began to gather together a good deal of random information about the country. 'Morocco is a protectorate, administered by the French in the name of the Sultan.' . . . 'In March, in the markets of Marrakesh, potatoes cost 30 francs per kilo.' . . . 'Casablanca has the world's second largest swimming pool.' . . . 'Skis showing signs of use are admitted duty free.' . . . 'At Rabat, H. E. the Sultan shows himself to his people in great solemnity on Fridays.' . . . and so on. From the travel agents I received an endless succession of pamphlets with photographs—usually of fierce warriors on sand dunes, silhouetted dramatically against the evening sky.

Morocco is the most Westerly country practising the religion of Mohammed. Indeed its Arabic name, *El Moghreb el Aksa*, means, 'The land of the farthest west.' Its eastern border lies approximately due south of Bristol. Surprisingly, in spite of its position, it is one of the least 'European' of Mohammedan countries. Most of the major influences during its history, both religious and political, have come from the east along the Mediterranean seaboard of Africa. There has been remarkably little commerce of ideas across the Straits of Gibraltar; and even the French protectorate, which was established just before the First World War, has not greatly disturbed the traditional ways of life. In 1954, however, there were signs of increasing concern with the affairs of the modern world, and of increasing political awareness.

One of the organizations to which I wrote in the early days of planning, 'The Islamic Cultural Centre', advertised its function as the dissemination of information about the Mohammedan faith. Its director very kindly sent me a number of booklets on this subject. But a week later (can it have been a coincidence?), I received a batch of political propaganda pamphlets telling of the evils of the French administration. Some of the titles, and contents, were hair-raising.

Gestapo in North Africa—Revelations of Tortures Under the French Administration.

Prostitution and the White Slave Traffic in 'French' North Africa.

Thirteen Systems of Torture.

There was a quotation from an article by Mr William O. Douglas, Associate Justice of the United States Supreme Court:

'1 July, 1954, a French police car, cruising slowly through a bazaar in Casablanca, suddenly opened fire on innocent Moors in the market place. These Moors were not fleeing or resisting arrest. They were shopping peacefully . . . three died; three were hurt. French terror was teaching the Moors a lesson.'

I had not been interested in Moroccan politics, but these pamphlets caused me some concern. Whether they were true or false, it was clear that all was not well. The tracts had not mentioned violence on the part of the Moors, but I began to notice small items in the newspapers, telling of riots in the larger towns, of bomb explosions and strikes.

A college friend of mine had visited Morocco that summer. He had been stranded without money in Casablanca, and spent a week in the

Arab quarter, sleeping in a disused truck and living entirely on dates. During his stay the newspapers reported severe riots. He had noticed nothing.

I continued with my preparations.

The first major problem to be solved was that of transport. There were many possibilities. One could fly there, of course, or go by ship. It was even possible to travel by train, with a short sea trip across the Straits of Gibraltar. Each of these possibilities was considered in turn— and dismissed: flying because of expense, boat and train because of difficulties in transportation beyond the dock or railhead. Clearly the expedition ought to be independent of the vagaries of local transport. It must have its own vehicle.

My imagination ran riot. If we had a vehicle we need not restrict ourselves to one place. I began to collect information about Algeria, even Tunisia. Then I heard that the Algerian coast offered ideal conditions for underwater exploration. If we took diving equipment with us we might study the marine fauna. I co-opted Richard Cleave, a friend in college who had done some skin-diving in Malta. We journeyed together to visit the works of Siebe Gorman Ltd, makers of aqualungs, where one of their managers helped us to draw up a list of necessary equipment. We enrolled in the British Sub-Aqua Club, and wallowed in the Chelsea Baths with breathing tubes and cylinders of compressed air. We wrote to Algiers to ensure that we could get our cylinders re-filled on the spot. We read avidly the works of Commandant Cousteau and Hans Hass, considered the dangers of going down too deep, staying down too long. We discussed hotly the relative merits of different designs of spring-guns and of waterproof cameras. In fact, we had developed, while still on dry land, '*l'ivresse des grandes profondeurs*'.

Meanwhile, our plans for the truck had become equally grand, involving a 10,000 mile run through Morocco, Algeria and Tunisia. We intended to average a hundred miles a day for more than three months. At the same time we hoped to collect animals along the route. I think we must have regarded animal collecting as a series of intermittent ten-minute dashes with a butterfly net. We certainly cannot have considered the possibility that the truck might break down.

By this time the first meeting of the Expedition Council was close at hand. We typed out an impressive document which was headed, *A Proposed Expedition to North Africa*, and which gave details of our scheme. The council met to consider it and, wisely enough, turned it down. They pointed out that we were expecting to travel too far in too short a time, and doubted whether the collection of insects would justify the expense of such a trip. We were told also that there were a number of people already studying the undersea life of the Mediterranean, and that they had far more extensive diving facilities than we could hope for. They were, moreover, established on the spot, not mere visitors for a brief period.

Had not the council's disposal of our plans been so crushingly logical, I might well have abandoned altogether the idea of going to Morocco. As it was, I became mulishly determined to carry it through. Vanity was hurt, and demanded recompense. I gambled on being able to produce a really businesslike proposal for the council's final meeting.

With this in mind, I decided to restrict our activities to Morocco, and to abandon the idea of underwater exploration. Other subjects for study must be included, as well as zoology. Suitable people must be found to carry them out—people who were not only good at their subject, but were also capable of getting along with each other under the irritating conditions of an expedition.

I took the selection of personnel seriously. I had heard many stories of parties which set out, well organized and with excellent intentions, whose programmes had been ruined by quarrels and disagreements. When I noised it abroad in the university that I wanted suitable people to make up the party, there was a surprising number of applicants. I interviewed them pompously, taking advantage of the almost pathetic desire of some of them to embark upon an 'Adventure', and enjoying the unaccustomed feeling that I was an employer selecting employees. It speaks much for their good nature that they did not tell me to go to blazes.

From this batch of applicants, two people seemed to stand out above the others. The first of these was John Newbould, a first year botanist who had been an officer in the Commandos. He struck me immediately as a 'man of action', capable of making decisions on the spur of the moment. He had been in the desert during his National Service, and knew the problems of travel and subsistence in hot countries.

The second was Humphrey Beckett, almost the reverse of John, less practical but more imaginative, more interested in motives than in actions. He had spent the previous summer walking across Lapland. He was reading History, and was interested in the habits and customs of primitive peoples.

With Humphrey and John in the party I felt more confident. It was good to be in company again, for Richard had decided that the trip, without underwater diving, was not for him.

John, with his knowledge of the desert, was put in charge of equipment and transport. Humphrey, who had a flair for languages and diplomacy, would contact the Moroccan authorities, arrange visas, book tickets, and so on. I was to co-ordinate our several activities—and raise money.

This was no easy matter. So much depended upon whether or not the Expedition Council would give their approval. I had to assume that they would. I wrote letters:

Dear Sir,

We are planning an expedition to Southern Morocco. We hope to have the support of Oxford University and the Royal Geographical Society. I wondered if you might possibly be able to help us. . . .

Such letters were sent to every organization which might contribute to an expedition. There were many refusals, but we did get support. The Grocers' Company very kindly offered us £20. A number of colleges contributed. The *National Geographical Magazine* gave us £100 in advance for an article. We opened an Expedition Account, and felt that we were really getting under way.

Meanwhile, we added another member to the party. Colin Pennycuick was a zoologist, due to take his degree that year. He was something of a Bohemian, oblivious of personal discomfort, devoted to his subject, but with a wide knowledge of other topics. He had already taken part in two expeditions, and we learned to appreciate him as an almost ideal travelling companion. He was delegated to arrange our food supplies, a duty which he carried out with great efficiency. At the same time he managed to gain a first-class degree in Zoology. He celebrated his success in characteristic fashion—by spending the night in a nearby wood, watching badgers.

Colin helped me to draw up the plan which we submitted to the Royal Geographical Society. It was two days before the closing date when we discovered that applications were due. Late that night I called at his lodgings. His landlady kept a dog, and life in the house centred upon that fragrant animal. We crept quietly up the stairs, not to preserve the sleep of his landlady (who slept well), but to avoid waking the dog (who did not).

Colin lived in a small bed-sitting-room—in a state of chaos. In order to sit down I had to remove several books, an old shirt, the skull of a dog, three photographs of sea birds, an exposure meter, and the chassis of a home-made wireless.

We worked through the night, drinking numerous mugs of black coffee to keep ourselves awake. . . .

This plan was certainly more practicable than the previous one. We were to visit only a restricted area in the Atlas Mountains of southern Morocco, an area which was little known because it fell under the jurisdiction of el-Glaoui, the Pasha of Marrakesh. As a reward for his help during 'the War of Pacification' in the nineteen twenties and thirties, the French Government had refrained from interfering in the administration of the Pasha's home territories. As a result of this the tribes in the vicinity of his *kasbah* (castle) at Telouet had preserved almost completely their traditional ways of life. They would thus be particularly interesting to Humphrey as an ethnologist. At the same time the region is very suitable for botanical and zoological researches. Lying across the spine of the main range of the High Atlas, it includes an area of climatic transition. On the northern slopes, which catch water-laden air blowing in from the sea, the climate is comparatively damp. It could roughly be described as 'Mediterranean'. The highest peaks, many of which are capped with snow throughout the whole year, have an alpine climate similar to that of mountains in southern Europe. But the south slopes of the Atlas, bordering on the Sahara, are desert—dry and hot. These three climatic zones occur within a few miles of each other, and result in a great profusion and confusion of plant and animal life. We hoped to compare plant, animal and human communities on the northern and southern slopes. On the peaks we expected to find isolated populations which were relics of past Ice Ages.

There were, too, a number of subsidiary projects: collections of pottery and coins, a study of agricultural techniques, the recording of folk-music, and the examination of human blood types. The last was to be carried out by Charles Pasternak, a school friend of mine who hoped to join us for a short while during his vacation.

It was four o'clock in the morning before we finished the plans. We felt that the result of our labours looked impressive. But would the Royal Geographical Society feel the same?

Perhaps they did. A few weeks later we heard that they had accepted our proposals, and would contribute £50 towards the expense of the trip. Furthermore, the Geographical Magazine Trust Fund would give us another £50 in advance for an article. Then, within two or three days, came the final meeting of the Expedition Council, and we learnt that they too had decided in our favour. Official permission to use the name of the university followed soon after. We were no longer merely four undergraduates with a plan—we had become 'The Oxford University Expedition to Southern Morocco'. Later on, signing cheques and documents, I came to regret the length of the title, but at this moment it seemed very important and impressive. At the same time I felt a little uneasy. I had enjoyed building castles in the air, but it was almost disconcerting to find them suddenly taking substance. There seemed to be endless things to do, and I wondered if we could ever complete them in time. I began, too, to read the reports of political disturbances in Morocco with a less courageous anticipation. All this, however, did not prevent me from taking an immodest delight in signing myself: 'Leader. O.U. Expedition to Southern Morocco.'

One of the greatest weaknesses of the party at this time was the lack of someone with a knowledge of geography and surveying, who could produce maps of the area we wished to study, and whose work would integrate our various activities in the field. We needed, too, a mechanic.

Peter Galloway filled the bill. He was reading Geography at Merton College and he had been an M.T. officer in the Cavalry. He was quiet, patient, and almost completely imperturbable. I felt that we would value his even temperament in times of stress. Such indeed proved to be the case. He became the fifth and final member of our group.

Now that our efforts were officially recognized, a number of firms very kindly offered to let us have their products free or at a reduced price. But, alas, there was not a car manufacturer amongst them. We still had to buy our truck.

John finally discovered one which seemed suitable, an ex-Army one-ton Canadian Ford. Since the war it had been used as an agricultural vehicle on the estates of the Marquess of Bath. It appeared to be mechanically sound, although the coachwork was by no means beautiful. We bought it for sixty-five pounds and returned to Oxford rejoicing.

We were very proud of our new acquisition, and drove about in it on every possible occasion. It was a ponderous thing, but riding in the cab gave one a sense of tremendous power. It seemed impossible that anything could resist its progress, and indeed on the occasion when we were involved in an accident (which removed the entire mudguard of a parked car) we were unable to find even a scratch upon its steel-clad sides.

There were many modifications needed before it would be fit for desert travel; a condenser on the radiator to prevent loss of water, a double roof to keep off the heat of the sun, a canvas back, special all-weather tyres, a sand-filter for the carburettor—and so on. In addition we planned a bench seat to accommodate three people in the front, seats in the back for the other two members of the party, and a roof-rack over the cab to take jerrycans of water and fuel.

The engine was completely overhauled by a local garage. We gathered together spares and tools of every description. We informed ourselves of all the ills that trucks are heir to. At first I hardly knew a distributor head from a connecting rod, but soon I was learnedly discoursing with mechanics on tappets and big ends and differentials. Peter, of course, already knew about such things. It was just as well.

Meanwhile, we were assembling the rest of the equipment. My room, much to the despair of the landlady, began gradually to fill up with a large and heterogeneous collection of objects. One armchair came to house ten boxes of penicillin, two prismatic compasses, a small hatchet, forty feet of rope, and a large supply of toilet paper. The other groaned under a seventy-six pound crate of tinned margarine. Beneath the desk huddled bottles of antiseptic and tins of foot powder. Heaped in a corner were six pair of suède boots. The floor was scattered with bills, letters, forms, and stacks of impressively embossed stationery.

Chaos was nothing new to Colin, but now his room was cluttered with cases of tinned meats, bottles of vitamin tablets, sauces and preserves. From time to time a delivery man would appear to add to the confusion with 120 lb. of biscuits, or fifty-six 'Ready Dinners'. John was no better off, for he housed the camping and cooking equipment. Peter, however, fared worst of all. When the time came for packing, we assembled *everything* in his rooms in Merton. It was an expedition in itself to reach the bed.

Packing was no simple matter. The gear had to be stowed in such a way that it could easily be transported by pack mule when we reached the end of our journey. A solution was found in the use of champagne boxes; a convenient size, since one could be slung on each side of a mule. Thus our equipment came to be packed in a series of containers, each with a large label reading *Moët & Chandon*. This gave rise to some caustic comments about what we considered to be essential supplies.

As the time for our departure drew near things became more and more hectic. There was a national rail strike which caused last-minute delays in the delivery of our equipment, and I hurried about trying to arrange for transport by road. There were complications, too, about John's passport. He was born in India, and the Foreign Office would not issue him with the passport unless he could show his birth certificate. This involved a long correspondence with the registrar of some remote Indian township, and wasted valuable time.

Then we suffered a really grave setback. The engine of our truck started to produce a sinister knocking noise, and the garage diagnosed it as big-end trouble. This was less than a week after the vehicle had been passed as mechanically perfect. We worried whether the repairs could be completed in time for us to leave England on 30 June.

The repairs were at last finished, but the cost was a crippling blow to our finances.

One of the Cambridge expeditions had written a book about their experiences. It was called *Into the Blue*. I decided that we also should write one, but entitle it *Into the Red*.

There were other problems. We discovered, for instance, that we had asked for the wrong size of tyres for the truck, and when they arrived we could not fit them to the wheels.

One by one the difficulties resolved themselves. The rail strike ended, the passport came through, and at the last minute the Goodyear Company delivered the proper tyres. It was a dramatic delivery, for they were obliged to load them into a small van and to drive at high speed from Wolverhampton to Oxford.

We were almost ready to go. There remained only the packing of our equipment, and we assembled in Peter's rooms, which were by now completely filled with piles of boxes. The packing took several days and most of the intervening nights.

On one of these occasions Peter was away in London, and Humphrey had been working so late that he decided to sleep in Peter's bed. The next morning a servant appeared to wake the sleeping figure. He was expecting, no doubt, to find Peter, and it must have been a shock for him to discover a complete stranger. But college 'scouts' are famous for their imperturbability. He merely said:

'Good morning, sir. I would not, if I were you, appear at breakfast.'

We had arranged to have most of our boxes sealed by the officers of the Customs and Excise in Oxford. We made lists of their contents in several languages. The sealing ceremony started late one afternoon; the Customs officer arrived at six o'clock. He checked through the contents of each box. Then we nailed it shut, so that he could bind the box with steel tape and set his seal upon it.

When the business was completed we suddenly realized that it was extremely late, so late in fact that the gates of Merton College had finally closed. There was only one thing to do. We would have to escort our Customs officer over the college wall. It seemed a suitably bizarre beginning for our enterprise; to be smuggling out an excise man at dead of night!

The following day we borrowed a weighing machine from my college bathroom and calculated the total weight of the boxes. It came to 3,300 lb. The capacity of the truck was given as 2,200, but we discovered that Government vehicles were always rated at a lower capacity than they were capable of supporting. We kept our fingers crossed.

On the night of 29 June I did not get a great deal of sleep, and the following morning my landlady wakened me early.

'You're going to Morocco today, aren't you?' she said; 'I'll make you some sandwiches.'

CHAPTER THREE

'Tartarin' Moves

Travel with them, and understand them.
Men show themselves during journeys.

MOROCCAN PROVERB

WE assembled by the truck in Merton Street and Charles Pasternak came to photograph our departure. He took several shots of us sitting and standing on the bonnet of the cab. Then we were away, round the corner, down the High Street, past the colleges. No one took any notice. We drove along the London Road, the tyres humming on the tarmac and the wind blowing through the open windows of the cab. We stopped briefly to pick up spares at a garage on the other side of London, then hurried on once more to Dover. Peter was at the wheel, John and I squeezed into the front seat, Humphrey and Colin were in the back. It was dark when we arrived and we set up our first camp on a bombed site overlooking the sea.

Just before I went to sleep I remembered that, for purposes of documents, I had registered our vehicle as being coloured light grey. We had intended to paint it so that its metal sides would reflect the heat of the sun, and so that in Morocco we would not be mistaken for a military expedition. But here we were in Dover and the truck was still its original khaki. The ferry to France left on the following morning at 11 a.m., so we got up at first light, bought some pots of quick-drying cellulose paint and, in the course of four hours, transformed our truck. It looked magnificent. We stuck a university shield on the radiator grill and John painted the expedition's titles on one of the doors. We drove into the Customs shed with clear consciences; the truck now matched its description.

We had no trouble with the Customs, for the official in Oxford had done his work well. Humphrey, when inquiring into the formalities of travel, had discovered that the only two articles upon which we would have to pay export duty were a half shaft and some cheese. We abandoned the half shaft and hid the cheese.

We were obliged to park the truck in the lower part of the ferry, among the railway carriages, since it was too large to be admitted to the car deck. The sea was calm and we arrived at Dunkirk in the early afternoon, driving down the railway lines to the French Customs.

A *douanier* inspected the truck.

'It will be necessary,' he said, 'to pay a fee of 14,000 francs.'

'But the French Embassy told us nothing of this.'

'I am sorry, but it is necessary."

'We can't pay.'

'Then I shall not allow you to land.'

At 9 p.m. we were still in Dunkirk. I sat at the edge of the water looking out over the docks, watching huge cranes unloading ships. They looked like a colony of Praying Mantises. John spent the time completing the lettering on the door. Colin was sketching the harbour. Peter and Humphrey had been closeted in the Customs office for over an hour, arguing about the fee. It would be depressing, I thought, to be forced to return so soon. Everyone on the dock seemed to be moving —except us. We brewed tea on the Primus by the dockside.

Peter and Humphrey had no success with the *douanier* but eventually it was agreed that we should visit the British Vice-Consul. Humphrey and I were driven out of the docks in a small van. It was now quite late. At the barrier the guard challenged the van, and came round to the back, shining a torch on our faces.

'So,' he said to our French companion, 'you are trying to help the English to escape.'

He looked determined and ferocious, and I was worried—until I suddenly realized that he was very drunk. We placated him and moved on.

The Vice-Consul was not at home and we returned to the Customs for another argument. We told them we were quite ready to stay on their dock until they let us out, we had our food with us. Eventually they despaired and, taking our names and addresses, allowed us to continue the journey.

On the first of July we were cheerful and optimistic as we bowled breezily along the roads of northern France. The truck was performing well, life was good, and in ten days we would be at our destination.

I was thinking beautiful thoughts: How lucky we were to have bought such a splendid vehicle! The noise of the engine, I felt, sounded so powerful, so dependable. But I was wrong.

'Listen,' said Peter, 'can you hear a peculiar knocking noise?' There
was indeed a faint but unmistakable 'tap-tap-tap'.

'Big-ends,' he said.

This was serious. A man told us that there was a good Ford agent at
Evreux, the next town on the road. We treated the truck with elaborate respect until we reached the garage. The agent was confident
that he could effect a repair, and we wandered round Evreux while he
and Peter performed prodigious feats of mechanical surgery. We sat in
a café watching the bustle of Evreux and wondering whether we
would ever get to Morocco.

But the truck was repaired, and by 3 July we had passed Bordeaux
and were approaching the Spanish frontier. There had been no further
complications, except for the occasion, near St Maure, when someone
had let in the clutch too vigorously, and all our equipment—boxes,
stoves and cases—was scattered over the road. It was raining then, and
by the time we had repacked the truck our tempers were frayed.

We were beginning to get on each other's nerves, and petty quarrels
became more and more frequent. Peter, however, was patient and
imperturbable; Colin ventured only an occasional sarcastic remark.
The main offenders were John, Humphrey, and I.

John had always claimed that he 'did not suffer fools gladly'. Humphrey and I felt offended that he should include us in this category. No
doubt he was quite justified, for we were both incompetent when it
came to the practical details of communal life. We took longer than
the others to light the cooking stoves, to erect the camp beds or to
pack up our belongings.

It is not that our domestic arrangements were complicated. After the
first night, we gave up the erection of tents, and slept out under the
stars. If it rained we would cover ourselves with a tarpaulin. This exposed existence had only one disadvantage; from time to time we
would wake up in the morning to find ourselves surrounded by local
inhabitants, who would watch with interest while we dressed. I became
experienced at putting on my clothes while still in bed.

We drove south over the Garonne and through the forests of Bordeaux, to the French frontier post at Hendaye. On the other side of
the border at Irun was the Spanish Customs. The officials were suspicious; but we were prepared. We carried a letter from the Spanish
Embassy in London. It was headed by an embossed coat of arms and
stamped with impressive seals. It had an electric effect, and we were

ushered through without difficulty. At lunch time we stopped briefly in San Sebastian, a city which impressed our bachelor party by the beauty of its women. We were tempted to linger but, bristling with virtue, pushed on beyond Vittoria, where the truck broke down. It must be said to its credit that it selected a delightful spot in which to do so, for we stopped in the mountains, within ten yards of a spring where water welled up into a stone trough. We were above the tree line and all around us the gently rolling hills were covered with short grass and small alpine flowers. We washed in the fountain trough and before bed Humphrey and I walked to a little village not far away. It was very small, three or four houses and a minute church, but it was a pleasant place on that clear evening. We came back almost glad that the truck had stopped.

Peter discovered the trouble, a fault in the distributor, early the following morning, and we proceeded south through Burgos.

That afternoon we halted for a while to collect animals and plants. John was digging with his sheath-knife when a small urchin turned up to watch. John said to Colin, 'You ought to take a photograph of him,' and pointed at the boy with his knife. The child clearly thought that he was being threatened. He became frightened, and screamed for his father, who was working in a nearby field. The man advanced, shouting streams of voluble Spanish, and we stood mute while he castigated us. It was perhaps as well that we could not understand a word. The small boy stood in the background, clutching a large scythe and feeling, no doubt, very brave. We drove off, embarrassed, hoping that misunderstandings of this sort would not occur in Morocco.

Some way further on we stopped for dinner beside some low scrubby oaks. Afterwards the vehicle would not start. We spent the night 'getting the truck into really good shape'. Then in the morning we started at the top of a hill, rolled in full sail to the bottom, and stuck. We had travelled exactly half a mile.

Peter spent the next four hours underneath the truck trying to discover what was wrong. Humphrey and I sat in the back chatting idly. Humphrey had been reading the works of Alphonse Daudet, and he felt that we had much in common with one of his heroes, Tartarin de Tarascon, who set out with great expectations to hunt big game in North Africa, but who achieved nothing. We decided to name the truck 'Tartarin'. The others also thought it appropriate and we painted the title in large red letters along the front mudguard. Peter laboured on as the sun rose higher and higher. The heat was oppressive and we became irritable. John and I had a heated argument about something trivial.

Our quarrels were now becoming worse than ever and I wondered if the party would disintegrate even before we reached our goal. The continual breakdowns were tremendously irritating and we still had not learned to live in peace with one another. This particular argument seemed to be working up to a climax when deliverance came. We were surprised to see an ancient London taxicab sedately rolling along the dusty Spanish road. I waved, and it stopped. We were even more surprised when four very attractive girls climbed out. Everybody immediately became affable and tea was brewed with lightning speed.

'Never underestimate the power of a woman,' I thought.

The girls were Canadians, celebrating their graduation from college by driving through Europe. They had bought the antique taxi in London and had already covered several thousand miles. They showed us cuttings from an English newspaper which told of their trip. They were going to Madrid and we arranged to meet them there. After their departure the truck was repaired within half an hour and we set off in pursuit. We soon overtook them, but we ourselves were overtaken when the truck slowed on a steep hill. The affair developed into a race, but eventually they left us behind, because we stopped at the summit of a pass for our first meal in a restaurant. We went on in the dark to camp on a grass-covered hill about three miles from Madrid.

On the morning of 7 July we arrived in the capital. The girls had got there before us. We knew this because we saw their taxi parked in one of the streets, but although we searched diligently we did not find them. Colin and I spent most of the day wandering around the Prado, enthralled by its magnificent collection of paintings, its monumental El Grecos and terrifying Goyas.

The journey south from Madrid was uninterrupted by breakdowns and we made very good time over the Castilian Plain. It was blisteringly hot and at midday we stopped for a siesta under some trees by the roadside. It was impossible to sleep for the noise of cicadas chirruping on the branches. Two Spanish civil guards joined us under the trees and shared our tea, a beverage which they obviously did not enjoy.

*   *   *   *

On 9 July we passed through Granada and reached the Mediterranean coast. Here the road crawled round enormous cliffs, which dropped several hundred feet to the sea. The road surface was extremely rough, some of the corners were very sharp, and it was impossible to see a vehicle approaching from the other direction. It was altogether a frightening drive. We passed two accidents in a stretch of about six miles, but in both cases the vehicles had driven into the rock rather than over the edge. In spite of the hazards the scenery was superb and one could look down from time to time on small coves where villages lay in the shelter of the great cliffs. We drove down a steep, winding track to one of them.

There were twenty or thirty white-washed houses scattered irregularly along a single dusty road, the road led down to a beach where fishing nets were drying in the sun. I do not think that the village had many visitors. Our arrival caused a sensation, and the whole population turned out to look at the peculiar foreigners. They crowded round the truck, staring at us, but saying nothing. It felt like the first night of a bad play. We went into an inn for drinks, and the crowd followed us until the big, bare room was packed with silent people. Sitting at a rough wooden table we drank inferior sherry from dirty glasses. Flies buzzed in the stuffy room. Our audience stared and stared. It was an unnerving experience, and we soon fled back to the truck—and the main road.

'Tartarin' was still behaving itself; we passed Malaga before nightfall, and the next morning approached the Rock of Gibraltar.

The contrast between the sloppily-clad soldiers on the Spanish side and the smart 'bobbies' who controlled the traffic at the British border was a heartening one. But our spirits were damped again by a very efficient Customs examination. We had bought a single bottle of wine from Spain and we were told to pay duty on it. We solved the problem by drinking it on the spot. Our shotguns were confiscated. They would apparently be returned when we left 'The Rock'. Beyond the Customs post the road crossed the single runway of Gibraltar's airfield and we had to wait while a four-engined transport took off. We drove through the narrow streets of the almost incredibly compact town to a square outside the Convent, residence of the Governor.

We had been given a letter of introduction to the Governor and because we did not intend to stay long in Gibraltar, I decided to get it to him as soon as possible. I approached one of the soldiers at the gate and told him that I wished to make an appointment to see His Excellency. The soldier regarded me suspiciously, and indeed he was justified in doing so. I was dressed in my oldest clothes, covered with the dust of Spanish roads and the grime from an oily truck. He eventually decided to lead me to an office which housed one of the Governor's orderlies. I explained my business.

'The Governor's very busy, you know', said the orderly, 'and he may not be able to see you within the next few days.' I expressed disappointment.

'But he's free now. He's having his tea at the moment.'

'I can't possibly call on him now, dressed as I am.'

'Oh, I'm sure he won't mind.'

'No, I can't possibly do that. I'll just leave the letter and hope that he can see me some other time.'

'I'm sure this will be your only opportunity, sir.' We argued for some time and eventually, I regret to say, he persuaded me. The orderly took me through a cool patio and up some stairs. He knocked on a door.

'A gentleman to see you, sir,' he said.

The Governor must have been surprised at the dishevelled object which entered his sitting-room, but he was very kind—in spite of my precipitate and bad-mannered intrusion. He offered me tea and I perched uncomfortably on the edge of a sofa, hoping that I would not leave a patch of oil behind me.

He had an engagement in a few moments, he said, but he told his orderly to put a guest room at our disposal, so that we could wash and brush up. I thanked him and departed.

The guest room was palatial and we luxuriated in the comfort of hot baths, after which the batman served us a mammoth tea.

Our first call after tea was at the hospital where we were given antityphoid injections. We had already had one set of these in England, but the second injection must be given two weeks after the first, and we did not have time for both before we left.

We wandered around the streets of the town and found, near the aerodrome, that a fair was in progress; a fair with bumper-cars, roundabouts, ferris wheels and coconut shies. At one end rows of chairs were laid out in front of a rostrum, and here we saw the Governor again, giving away the prizes for the annual tennis tournaments. We did not hear his speech, and even the people in the front row seemed to have difficulty in doing so. The noise from the fair overwhelmed it completely.

After sunset we drove through a tunnel cut in the rough rock to the eastern beach. We set up our camp-beds on the gravel strand, below the great concrete catchments which trap fresh water for the town.

All of us, when we woke in the morning, had high temperatures— and tempers. They were the result of our final typhoid injections. Peter went off to see the Governor's Military Secretary, who arranged for our truck to go into Capurro's garage.

Perhaps it was the effect of the injections, but on the way to the garage, in one of the narrow streets that climb up the lower reaches of the Rock, we ran into a parked car. The car was dented severely, but 'Tartarin' was unscathed.

We found board and bed that night at the Merchant Navy Home. It was a marvellous comfort to sleep once more in a real bed—the first time we had done so since leaving Oxford.

The garage worked on the truck throughout the following day, and we occupied ourselves wandering about Gibraltar. Colin and I climbed to the top of the Rock to look out over the little town and to get our first glimpse of the coast of Africa. Colin took a dramatic photograph of me looking out towards Morocco. Some time later we discovered that I had been looking in the wrong direction, and that the rugged cliffs at which I was gazing were, in fact, in Spain.

In the evening Peter and I wandered down Main Street and visited one of its many 'night-clubs'. It was a harsh, bare place, clearly designed for the entertainment of visiting sailors, and its only major attraction was a sad collection of over-painted, over-age hostesses. A bored band churned out dance music. Two of the harpies attempted to attach themselves to us.

'We come and sit at your table, yes?'

'No.'

'Why not?' asked the uglier of the two. 'You no like me?'

'No.'

The lady spat, and departed to a distant table, but from time to time she glared at me vindictively across the room.

On 13 July, an ominous date, we caught the one o'clock ferry to Tangier.

CHAPTER FOUR

El Moghreb el Aksa

He that travelleth into a country before he hath some entrance into the
language, goeth to school, and not to travel.

FRANCIS BACON

THE car ferry, *Mons Calpe*, is a credit to British Enterprise. It is
modern, clean and comfortable; the service is courteous; the
arrangements for moving vehicles are carried out with speed and
efficiency. In fact it has all the virtues which we failed to find on the
British Railways vessel from Dover to Dunkirk, though it must be
said in the defence of the latter that the *Mons Calpe* deals with a much
smaller volume of traffic.

The day was bright as we left the jetty at Gibraltar. There was an
American carrier berthed nearby, and the sun flashed from the smooth
metal surfaces of the aircraft lying huddled on its decks. The little town
looked gay, slightly defiant of the huge precipices of rock which tower
above it. Spanish fishing-boats dipped ahead of us in the fresh breeze.

As we churned through the blue straits, Colin and Peter and I stood
on the rail looking out towards the shores of Africa. We felt elated, for
after all the troubles of the journey we were approaching our objective.
I had even stopped quarrelling with John.

There was a man near us also looking out towards the coast of
Morocco. He turned and caught sight of Colin.

'Weren't you at Wellington?' he asked.

Colin gaped, and then remembered him. They had indeed been at
school together. This event occasioned a long discussion on meeting
people in unlikely places. Colin and I made a bet that at the end of our
journey, somewhere in the Atlas, we would meet at least one man
from Oxford.

Within two hours we were sailing smoothly into the harbour at
Tangier, and speculating about the Perils and Dangers of the African
continent.

But Tangier is not Africa, not in spirit or appearance. The white perpendicular buildings along its modern sea-front could belong to any Mediterranean holiday resort. It is clean and tidy, and there is no hint of its reputation as a city of dark intrigue. The smugglers and crooks and spies, if indeed they live there, must inhabit antiseptic suburban villas. There is certainly some local colour to be found in Tangier, in the Gran Socco, or in the alleys of the old town, but one feels almost that it is preserved for the benefit of romantically-minded visitors. This, of course, is not true, for Tangier is the home of many thousands of Moroccans; but the impression remains that it is a predominantly European city.

The impression is to some extent justified, for it has been occupied by Europeans for 1,000 out of the last 2,000 years of its history. Reputedly founded by the son of Neptune, Tangier was controlled first by the Phoenicians, then by the Carthaginians, and later by the Romans. In Roman times it became, under the name of Tingis, the capital of Tingitane (Morocco), and for 400 years it knew peace and prosperity, until in the fifth century A.D. it was overcome by the Vandals. Some years later the Visigoths occupied it and reduced the Roman city to ruins. In A.D. 682 Okba ben Nafd captured Tangier, and for the first time it became a Muslim city. During the following 900 years it was contested by the Mohammedans of both Spain and Morocco, and it finally passed into the hands of the latter.

In 1471 Tangier was captured by the Portuguese, and thereafter it was alternately in Spanish and Portuguese hands until in 1661 it came under English rule, as part of the dowry of Catherine of Braganza to King Charles II. England's first commissioner in her new possession was Samuel Pepys, and he revisited the town in 1683 as secretary to the Admiralty.

Tangier was abandoned by the British under the attacks of the megalomaniac Sultan Moulay Ismail, but not before Charles II had received a special emissary from the Sultan—an emissary which, with its gifts to the king of two lions and thirty ostriches, and its colourful manners, was the talk of England in 1682. Anthony Wood, the Oxford antiquary, described their visit to the university.

'May 30th, Tuesday. About 8 of the clocke at night came into Oxford Hamet Ben Hamet Ben Haddu Ottur, Embassadour from the Emperour of Morocco and put in at the Angell Inn within East gate. Where being settled, the Vice chancellor and Doctors in their scarlet, with the bedells before them, congratulated his arrival.'

More than two hundred and fifty years later, in a lesser degree, we were returning the visit—as official representatives of Oxford University in Morocco. We did not arrive with such ceremony, but drove off the docks with 'Tartarin' making sinister internal noises. A hundred yards from the docks, we heard an enormous bang. We jammed on the brakes and jumped out to investigate. We discovered that four small boys had let off a fire-cracker underneath the truck. They approached, grinning.

'We show you round the city? Very good guides. Very cheap.'

Tangier was obviously the home of enterprise, even if it did not greet us with 'Doctors in their scarlet'.

We drove to the Consulate to report our arrival, and there Mrs Dunlop, the British Vice-Consul, very kindly offered to let us sleep on her veranda. She entertained us lavishly during our stay in Tangier: there were picnics on the Atlantic beaches by Cap Spartel, the extreme north-west point of the African continent; there were cocktail parties and visits to the town.

Our stay in Tangier had a wonderful effect on the morale of the party. It was a relief no longer to be cooped up together in the irritating confines of the truck. We stopped quarrelling and each decided that the others were really quite pleasant people, that we might even reach our objective and achieve some of the things we had set out to do. We quarrelled again after Tangier, but never with such intensity as during the first part of the journey. The 'rough edges' had been knocked off, and we began to appreciate each other's peculiar brands of humour; John's exuberant enjoyment of a situation, Colin's dry wit, and Humphrey's devious subtleties. I have omitted Peter, because we all appreciated him from the very first. He had always been straightforward and cheerful.

Tangier's outwardly suburban appearance was to some extent counteracted by the fantastic variety of nationalities which lived in it. Some had come there to evade the income-tax, some no doubt for more sinister reasons. Many were involved in the governments of Tangier, for it was ruled by an International Committee of Control, formed from representatives of Great Britain, Holland, the United States, France, Spain, Portugal, Belgium and Italy; a Committee of Control which was set up when the rest of Morocco was annexed by the French. At that time a number of countries felt that no one power should have sovereignty over Tangier, and that international control

was the only means by which this could be avoided. Britain was particularly in favour of the plan, lest the strategic value of Gibraltar should
be prejudiced.

Tangier had been described as a 'diplomatocracy'. All the power was
in the hands of the diplomats. The régime had its disadvantages, since
every member of the committee felt responsible not only for the best
possible administration of the city, but also for the interests of his own
country. Tangier was a free port, there was no income-tax, and the
administration was largely financed by the 13½ per cent levied on all
goods entering the Zone. Fully two-thirds of the total revenue of the
International Zone came from Customs.

We spent a good deal of our time in the Zone finding out more
about conditions of travel in Morocco, and through Mrs Dunlop we
met many people who knew the country well, including Peter Mayne,
author of *The Alleys of Marrakesh*. He had lived for a year in the *medina*
(old city) of Marrakesh, had taught himself Arabic, and had come to
know the day-to-day life of poor Moroccans. He told us about the
observances of Moorish society; how many cups of mint-tea to drink,
the correct forms of address to persons of different rank, the method of
eating *kus kus*—and so on.

*   *   *   *

On 16 July we entered Spanish Morocco. At the frontier post of
Cuesta Colorado the transition from the well-kept roads of Tangier to
the rutted tracks of Spanish Morocco was very noticeable. We felt that
in leaving the sophistication of Tangier we had left Europe. This at last
was Africa: the Spanish had done little to change the face of their part
of the Moroccan Protectorate.

We passed small groups of stone huts sheltering families of poor
natives. Cloaked figures strode along the roadside or sat hunched on
overloaded pack-mules. Many of the men wore the broad floppy
straw hat favoured by Berbers of the Rif. From time to time we
passed a Spanish dwelling. The Spaniards seemed to live in almost as
much squalor as did the Moroccans. This may to some extent account
for the fact that the Spanish were generally more popular in Morocco
than the French; the social barriers were not so great.

Fifty miles south of Tangier we came upon the ruins of Lixus—a
great expanse of tumbled masonry spreading out beside the road. This
ancient town was first established by the Carthaginians and later it be-

came a Roman colony. The area is rich in archaeological remains, and many tombs have been discovered, both Carthaginian and Roman. Pottery, bronze statuary and vases of alabaster have also been found. Humphrey wandered delightedly among the ruins, and we had great difficulty in enticing him away from them. He told us that according to certain Latin authors the famous Garden of the Hesperides was situated near Lixus, in the valley of the river Loukos. It was here that Hercules was supposed to have stolen the golden apples, after a fierce battle with the dragon which guarded them. More modern historians, less romantically inclined, tell us that the golden apples were merely oranges, and that the dragon represented simply the meandering river Loukos, which was notably treacherous to shipping.

Just before midday we reached the modern French frontier post at Arbaoua, where an official warned us about ambushes. An account of the events which followed has already been given, in the first chapter.

*   *   *   *

Following our night with the circus at Port Lyautey, we set off early for Rabat and halted for breakfast in the suburbs of the town. Then we drove straight to the British Consulate-General. The Consulate stands in a commanding position looking over the river Bou Regreg and over the salt-marshes which line its banks. We were received by Madame Racine, an Englishwoman who was married to a Frenchman and who worked in the Consulate. She very kindly offered to let us camp in her garden—an offer which we accepted with pleasure. Madame Racine was very good to us during our four days in Rabat. The sudden arrival of five young men must have caused great disruptions in her domestic arrangements, but we heard nothing of them.

The European town of Rabat seemed a curiously isolated place, undisturbed by the troubles and frictions which convulsed the rest of Morocco. It was beautifully laid out, with wide avenues lined by palms, and fine modern buildings. The French are justly proud of it. The good arrangement of many Moroccan cities is directly due to the foresight of Marshal Lyautey, who subjugated Morocco and who was named its first Resident-General. It was he who decided that the new cities should not encroach upon the old. In Rabat he ordered a large boulevard to separate the modern capital from the *medina*. He organized an office for 'town planning' which, under his constant supervision, was responsible for laying out streets, placing public buildings and gardens, and ensuring that historical monuments were not destroyed.

Like many other Moroccan cities, Rabat has a history of Roman occupation. The town was known by the Romans as Sala, perhaps because of the salt-marshes which surround it. Sala later fell to the Berbers, but the port became silted and they abandoned it, founding a new city on the other side of the river, a city which they called Salé. This became one of the most important seaports in Morocco, and was the home of famous pirates, the 'Salley Rovers', who ventured even as far as the Bristol Channel on their marauding expeditions.

The town of Rabat was re-established by the Sultan Yacoub el-Mansour. The site had been used as a fortified camp by an order of Mohammedan knights. Such a camp was known as a Ribat, and Yacoub el-Mansour, when establishing the city, called it Ribat el Fath —the Camp of Victory, commemorating his success at Alarcos against the Castilians. Near the town he began the construction of an enormous mosque, the minaret of which was intended to surpass those of the Giralda at Seville and the Koutoubia at Marrakesh. Unfortunately he died before completing the work, and all that now remains is the base of his minaret, known as the tower of Hassan, which stands lonely among a few broken columns overlooking the river.

The site of the ancient Roman town of Sala is still visible among the ruins of Yacoub el-Mansour's Ribat. Later architects built upon these ruins, and during the thirteenth and fourteenth centuries constructed a fortified monastery, and the necropolis of several Merinid Sultans. It was one of these, Aboul Hassan, the Black Sultan, who in 1339 erected the great ramparts which today surround the area. The site is now known as *Chellah*—presumably a corruption of Sala.

Humphrey and I visited Chellah one evening, passing through the large ornamented gateway which leads into it. There is a legend that within the stonework of this gate is concealed King Solomon's ring— a talisman of great power which enables its owner to speak the languages of animals and to control the *djnun* (spirits). The interior of Chellah was a peaceful place, and we strolled through gardens to a little mosque, whose thin minaret rose above a courtyard where Roman statuary was displayed. In the shade of trees we came upon a sacred spring, whose stone surround was worn thin by the feet of pilgrims. The spring was supposed to concentrate the blessing of no less than seven *marabouts* (Muslim saints). Within it lay sluggish black eels, also sacred, which were reputed to have lived there since the building of Ribat el Fath. The largest of them is supposed to conceal a gold ring—another talisman—in its head. Humphrey and I were enthralled by the place, and stayed there until nightfall, when white-cloaked figures came silently down to the mosque like the ghosts of long-dead *marabouts*.

Our time in Rabat was largely occupied with visits to members of the French Administration, in order to obtain final permission to set up our camp in the Atlas, and to find out more about the conditions there. We were much helped by M. Gilloteaux, the Director of Information, and by M. Horlaville of the Institut Géographique Nationale, who supplied us with maps and aerial photographs. The British Consul-General and Mrs Freese-Pennyfather entertained us one evening to cocktails, and generously wrote us a letter of introduction to el-Glaoui, the Pasha of Marrakesh. The Pasha was well-disposed towards the English, probably because of his association with Sir Winston Churchill.

During our stay we wanted to visit the *medina* of Rabat, but everyone told us that we must not do so. It was now dangerous, they said, for Europeans to enter the *medinas* of any Moroccan town. Nationalist feeling was high, and it was impossible efficiently to police the narrow alleyways. We were disappointed, and wondered how we would ever get to know the Moors if we were to be cut off from them in European cities.

On our fourth day in Rabat we heard that there were more English people heading for the Atlas, and that evening we met them. Ernest Gellner was a Lecturer in Philosophy at London University, but in his spare time he had become interested in anthropology. He had spent the previous summer living with a Berber tribe in the mountains at a place called Zaouia Ahansal. This year he was returning to the same place, and he had brought his wife Susan with him. We sat up late talking of our various plans, and discussing the political situation in Morocco.

In order to understand the conflict between the French and the forces of Moroccan nationalism it is necessary to look back to the founding of the Protectorate in 1912. At this time the Sultan called upon the French to restore order in the country. Morocco was in confusion, and the majority of the tribes were at war with one another or had declared themselves independent of the Sultan. To save his throne he called in the French, who already exerted some influence in Morocco through the trading posts which they had established there. A treaty was signed between France and Morocco in March 1912, and on 24 May of that year General Lyautey was named Resident-General. A brilliant soldier and administrator, he succeeded in binding Morocco together under one rule. He subdued the tribes in a series of inspired military operations. He renovated the archaic systems of government, but at the same time he respected scrupulously the traditions of the country. He initiated the construction of ports and roads and railways; he revolutionized methods of agriculture. There can be no doubt that if the French had not come to Morocco in 1912 the country would still be in a state of conflict, disorganization and poverty.

The French had, however, far greater power than the word 'Protectorate' would lead one to believe. They completely controlled the administration, and although the Sultan could refuse to assent to proposed legislation, he had no power of initiative. Jurisdiction, apart from the machinery of Koranic law, was completely in the hands of the French. The Moroccans came to occupy only an insignificant number of posts in the Civil Service, mostly in the lower ranks. At Rabat there was a school for training them in administration, but it was not founded until 1950.

In 1930 the French initiated a *dahir* (decree) which restored to the Berber tribes their own traditional methods of justice. The French were still at this time fighting to subdue the Berbers, and this action helped them in their campaigns. But it caused hard feeling among the Arabs, since it meant that one half of Morocco was not subject to the Koranic law, and many religious leaders saw it as a threat to the Muslim faith. It was perhaps this popular protest against the Berber *dahir* which brought the Nationalist movement into being, and from then on it slowly gained support. The Nationalists were encouraged by Left-wing parties in France, by General Franco, at the time of the Spanish civil war, by the collapse of France during the Second World War, and by the Allied landings in North Africa in November 1942. It was at this time that the Nationalists formed themselves into a united party, the *Istiqlal*, which asked only that independence should be given to Morocco over a period of time. The French arrested several leaders of the party, and as a result there were riots in a number of towns.

In 1927 the Sultan, Sidi Mohammed Ben Youssef, Mohammed V, succeeded to the throne. To begin with he had given his support to the French, but as the years went by he increasingly favoured the Nationa-

list parties. It is said that he was much influenced by an interview with
President Roosevelt at Casablanca, when the President supported
Morocco's claims for independence.

In 1951 the Resident-General Juin had an interview with the Sultan,
and formally asked him to disavow Nationalism. At the same time
there were demonstrations by Berber tribesmen who swarmed into
Rabat, apparently threatening the Sultan's palace. Others paraded
through Fez. The French claimed that the demonstrations were spon-
taneous; the Nationalists declared that they were deliberately organized
by the French in collaboration with the francophile Pasha of Marrakesh.

In 1952 there were further demonstrations, counter-demonstrations,
strikes and riots. On 20 August, 1953 the Sultan was deposed and de-
ported, in response—according to the French—to the pressure of
Moroccan public opinion. One suspects in this case that Moroccan
public opinion was strongly represented by the Berber chieftains, for
the Berbers had always been less interested in Nationalism than the
Arabs.

Sidi Mohammed Ben Youssef was replaced by Sidi Mohammed Ben
Arafa, Mohammed VI, but it is probably true that Mohammed VI did
not have the confidence of the majority of Moroccans. The anniversary
of Ben Youssef's deposition, 20 August, became a day of national
excitement, a day on which strikes and rioting invariably occurred.
Morocco at the time of our arrival was in a very unsettled state.

We felt, in our discussion with the Gellners, that it was a mistake
of the French to allow the settlement of Morocco by colonists. So
many Frenchmen had moved into the country that Europeans in the
cities were employed in menial tasks alongside the Moors. For the
same work they were paid higher wages than their Muslim companions,
and this must have been a continual source of irritation. The French
workmen could not be expected to have an understanding of the
Arab's complicated codes of behaviour with respect to his neighbours,
and they must have offended him with their apparently clumsy approach to human relations. Again, the presence of successful French
farms scattered over the countryside naturally inspired the jealousy of
the native. Even if these farms had been built up with great effort
from previously infertile soil, the superficial impression remained that
the French had procured all the best farming land, and that by so doing
they had deprived the Moroccan of his birthright.

Ernest believed that nationalism among the Berbers would begin in
D

the Glaoua tribe, the tribe which we intended to visit. It would do so, he said, because the Glaoua were closest to the French. Being immediately subject to the Pasha of Marrakesh they were employed in his service, and they would come to know the French and to be jealous of their comparative riches.

* * * *

The day after our meeting with the Gellners we set out from Rabat for Beni Mellal, where we had arranged to pick up M'Barek, our interpreter. We certainly needed someone to translate for us: none of us could speak either Arabic or Berber.

When I was making the preparations for our trip, I decided that we should all learn Berber, but I could discover only one person in the British Isles who knew the language, and he spoke only the Tunisian dialect—so different from Moroccan Berber that a Tunisian and a Moroccan would fail completely to understand one another. It became clear that we would need at least one interpreter, and we were recommended to inquire from the headmaster of the Berber College at Azrou.

The Berber College was the leading high school in Morocco. It may have been the only one. I did not hear of any others—except, of course, the *medersas*, Muslim 'universities' which give instruction in religious studies and Arabic literature. These, though admirable in their way, do not provide the benefits of Western education. They do not teach mathematics or science or other languages. Azrou has a high reputation, but obviously only a very few Moroccans get the opportunity to attend it.

The headmaster wrote, suggesting Mouhsine M'Barek as an intelligent and capable young man who would be willing to interpret for us. He could speak fluent Arabic, Berber and French. His English was good. We corresponded with M'Barek and arranged to meet him in Beni Mellal, where his uncle lived. He would wait for us there.

We drove south-east from Rabat, across rolling, scrub-covered hills, past the sacred city of Boujad, until in the evening we descended to the plain of Tadla—quite flat and fiercely hot. The Tadla plain was being slowly transformed into a rich agricultural region, and a great dam had been built in the river which crossed it. Upon one bank of this river stood the town of Kasba Tadla, whose fort commanded the valley. The town, captured in 1913 by Colonel Mangin, was the point from which many French military operations were started during the subjugation of the Middle Atlas. On the opposite bank there was a huge monument to the memory of the French officers and men who fell between 1912 and 1933 in the Tadla region. From the base of its four high concrete pillars, where we set up our camp for the night, we could see a magnificent view of the river and of the city beyond. On a flat piece of ground immediately below the monument there were many little reed huts surrounded by thorn fences, or plantations of prickly pear. They were *noualas*, the homes of sedentary plain-dwellers.

We awoke early the following morning, and from our point of vantage we could see the settlement slowly coming to life. Little figures appeared in the thorn compounds to shake out carpets; columns of smoke showed that breakfast was being cooked; dogs barked. Then we saw men leaving their homes to go about the duties of the day. Several of them set off on shiny new bicycles. In one corner of the settlement some kind of altercation was in progress; people congregated in a little group, shouting and gesticulating. In another place a man was making mud-bricks, pouring an unpleasant mixture into a mould and then pressing it down to squeeze out the liquid.

It was a fascinating business sitting on the hill and watching through our binoculars the life of the people below, people who went about their tasks oblivious that they were being observed.

We dragged ourselves away from the observation post, cooked breakfast, and drove off to Beni Mellal.

This town is the centre of the Dir, a well-watered region which stretches to the foot of the Atlas mountains. Around it are plantations of trees, fields of grain, and rich gardens, all irrigated from the many springs which abound in the area. A large grove of olives encircles the town to the south and east, and we passed by its fringes as we drove to the centre of Beni Mellal.

Here in the Place de France we parked the truck, and waited for M'Barek. The *Place* was surrounded by white-washed buildings, beneath which were arcades of little shops. The centre of the square was cool in the shade of trees, and upon scattered benches citizens gossiped idly. Beni Mellal was not a particularly beautiful or interesting town. It was modern, and there was an unpleasing mixture of architectural styles. The principles of Marshal Lyautey seemed to have been forgotten. Moorish and French buildings were sandwiched next to each other, and the people who passed in the streets outside them were similarly heterogeneous. Perhaps it was as a result of this unhappy

proximity that Beni Mellal seemed to have about it an atmosphere of
tension and unease. There was friction, I felt, between the two races,
and this friction was stronger in Beni Mellal than in any other town
that we had visited. This was only an irrational feeling, but it was
probably a valid one. We learned in time to sense whether or not the
inhabitants of a particular place were well-disposed towards us. We
could tell from the way they looked at us. In Beni Mellal they looked
hard and cold.

There were one or two, however, who were not hostile. An old man
on crutches came up to us as soon as we parked in the square. He carried
a monkey on his shoulder. He had a merry eye and an ingratiating
manner. His merry eye settled acquisitively upon the pile of equipment
at the back of the truck, and while the others went off to get a drink, I
stood guarding it—to make sure that our friend did no more than look.
The old man, it appeared, was an *ancien militaire* who had served with
the *Goums*. He spoke sufficient French to ask for money and cigarettes.

He and I performed a little *pas de deux* which must have amused the
watchers in the square. He sidled towards the back of the truck; I
sidled between him and his objective. He tried to get round me; I
moved again to block his way. This went on for some time, interrupted
only by mutual expressions of goodwill.

Some time later Mouhsine M'Barek appeared on the scene. He was
a young man of about eighteen dressed in European clothes—black
trousers, open-necked shirt and sandals. Although in fact a Berber, he
had definitely Arab features, with a lean face, aquiline nose, large ex-
pressive eyes, and the almost feline grace of movement that is so
characteristic of the Semites. At first he was understandably shy in our
company, but later he held his own as an outspoken member of the
party. He was unashamedly Nationalist, and determined that we
should go home with 'the right ideas about Morocco'.

Before we left Beni Mellal he invited me to come with him to his
uncle's house where he was to pick up his belongings. He led me
through narrow streets to the market-place. There were many stalls
selling fruit and vegetables, and one of them belonged to his uncle, who
hailed us cheerfully and presented me with a handful of ripe figs. His
home was nearby, and we entered it through a low wooden door,
which led into a small courtyard. M'Barek brought me a stool on
which I waited while he collected his things, and I was pleasantly surprised when he brought a teapot, and brewed a refreshing drink of

mint-tea, which we drank from small glasses. Opposite us sat an old blind woman, carding wool. Her eyes were white and opaque from cataract, and she clearly did not feel the flies which walked unhindered across them. We returned to the truck with M'Barek's small brown suitcase and an enormous roll of bedding, which we perched precariously on top of our pile of boxes. We were off on the final stage of our journey to Marrakesh.

'Tartarin' was behaving well as we bowled busily down the dusty road, and M'Barek seemed impressed.

'This is a good truck,' he said, cheerfully.

We shuddered at this monstrous temptation of fate.

'I hope it does not hear you,' I remarked.

Ten minutes later we broke down.

Mercifully it was a minor fault, and we were soon continuing on our way across the monotonous plain. We passed through the little town of El Kelaa Des Srarhna, and came to the edge of the Haouz—the plain which surrounds Marrakesh. Here we saw the first mud *kasbahs* of the south; red forts with crenellated towers built by the tribes during times of insecurity. Around them were plantations of olives and fig-trees, of vines and palms. Finally we gained our first sight of the minaret of the Koutoubia pointing to the sky above the oasis of Marrakesh.

CHAPTER FIVE

Red City, White Castle

M ARRAKESH lay before us: Marrakesh, a red city in green palm
groves, shimmering in the heat. 'The Gateway to the Sahara';
'The Residence of the Great Pasha'. I recited these titles to myself—to make sure of being impressed. An arrival of this sort is so often
an anti-climax. But the first sight of Marrakesh was genuinely exciting.

The circumspect dusty road wound carefully through ranks of palm
trees. It carried an increasing stream of traffic: cars and carts, donkeys
and camels, men and women. All of them seemed to be staggering
under huge loads of merchandise. I remembered that we were approaching one of North Africa's greatest centres of trade. But there were also
soldiers, smart *Goums* in their colourful uniforms, and dishevelled
irregulars with the swinging stride of the born mountaineer.

A final turn in the road brought us to the mud-red walls of the city,
where there was a massive gateway. An armoured car stood guard
outside it. A soldier waved us to a halt.

'It is not permitted to enter the *medina*. There are "events". Europeans are being evacuated to the *Gueliz*.'

'Have many been killed?'

'I do not know. There was a lot of noise.'

The *Gueliz*, which is the European quarter of Marrakesh, is a poor
monument to French administration. The red stone buildings, although
they are laid out in broad avenues, are ugly and badly proportioned,
and they have that peculiar dinginess which is characteristic of so many
reconstructed towns in Metropolitan France.

We drove to the centre of the city, parked the truck, and sought out
a café. The waiter told us more about the riots.

'They happened this morning, during the visit of the Resident-
General. We Moroccans hope that the new Resident will be more
sympathetic to the Nationalists. He has already made changes in the
administration. But the Pasha does not like this. At dawn his mes-

sengers were about in the *medina* saying: "The Pasha forbids you to make demonstrations in favour of the Resident."

'But when General Grandval came, the people were carried away with enthusiasm and shouted, "Vive Grandval! Vive Grandval!" The Pasha's soldiers were there, and tried to stop them. A fight started. The French soldiers joined in—the rest is obvious.'

We finished our drinks and set out to find somewhere to sleep. This proved to be difficult, since all the cheap hotels were in the *medina* and we could not afford those in the *Gueliz*.

While we were searching, Humphrey discovered that his camera was missing. We decided that it must have disappeared in Beni Mellal. Could our friend the *ancien militaire* have been responsible? His hand must have been very quick. Humphrey determined to go back to Beni Mellal on the bus. He departed, taking M'Barek with him to interpret, and left us to continue the quest for sleeping quarters. Night was closing in, and we were becoming desperate. Somebody suggested the American Red Cross hostel, but from there we were turned away. 'I'm afraid foreigners are not allowed.'

We decided to drive out of the city and camp in the palm groves. It was dark when we found a suitable place, in a cultivated sandy clearing about two hundred yards from the road. We were soon squatting round the Primus stove, watching a bubbling pot. The flames roared, casting a faint light on the little circle. A myriad stars shone bright above the palm trees. Near at hand a voice struck up in song. It was a high, plaintive, wavering song, which seemed attuned to the noises of the night, properly humble beneath the great arch of the sky.

Now, as later, it was the night which brought home to me the strangeness of Morocco. In the daytime the senses were confused by the intensity of impressions; the sun's brightness washed out the colours of the Moroccan scene. My idea of the Romantic, too, was disturbed by the sight of sewing machines in a market, or taxicabs parked at a palace gate. But at night one saw only the shade of a minaret against the sky, or a flickering lamp in the market place. At night too, with the eyes dimmed, the ear became master of the senses. Moroccan music is so unlike our own that by itself it can create an atmosphere of mystery and unlikelihood.

The song seemed to grow louder, then suddenly it stopped, and a figure appeared out of the darkness. It was an old man.

'*Salaam-o-alikum,*' he said. 'Peace be unto you.'

'*Alikum-salaam,*' we politely replied, motioning him to sit down. But he waved his forefinger across his face, in a gesture of negation, and burst into a long stream of Arabic. He soon realized that we could not understand a word and, shaking his finger once more, he wandered off into the night. A few minutes later he returned with a young girl who, it appeared, could speak a little French.

'It is folly to sleep here,' she said; 'you will all be killed.'

We asked why, but her reply was not clear. She seemed only to repeat that we should all be killed. I explained that we were English, not French, and that we had nowhere to sleep: but I do not believe she understood what an Englishman was. She talked for a long time with the old man, then turned to us and said.

'The men will guard you tonight.'

With that, they departed, leaving us puzzled.

I was frightened. I have always envied those who can put personal hazard out of their minds, but I am a coward. At even a hint of danger, I waste a great deal of time and energy in imagining all the terrible things that *might* happen. I decided, in spite of a good deal of opposition from the others, that we should arrange ourselves in defensive positions. Colin was stationed on top of the truck, Peter slept in the cab, and John was underneath. I lay in the back, armed with a large (and probably ineffective) knife.

I slept little, but shifted about uncomfortably, straining my ears for sounds in the darkness. I heard the faint rustle of palm fronds, the croak of frogs in the irrigation ditches, and the sound of dogs barking in the distance. I looked out, from time to time, into the moon-bleached clearing.

I dozed—to awake suddenly. There were sounds of movement at the edge of the clearing. A dark shape showed up against the pale earth. Then it barked, and I went back to sleep.

Dawn came and we climbed out of the truck, hopping to restore the circulation in our cramped limbs. It was easy to laugh now at my ridiculous fears of the night before. Then the old man appeared with two companions. Had they been standing guard? We never discovered.

As the truck rumbled towards Marrakesh, camel caravans, which had spent the night outside the city walls, were getting under way for the final stage of their journey. Hooded figures were tightening loads on the backs of their beasts, while others brewed coffee or tea. The smoke from their fires rose straight in the cool morning air. The red ramparts of the *medina* towered above them. Our business lay within these walls, and although there were again many soldiers about we were allowed to enter.

Marrakesh is an ancient town, for it was founded in the year 1062 by the Emir Youssef Ben Tachfine, a Berber chieftain who came north from the Sahara to establish himself as ruler of all Morocco and first Sultan of the Almoravid dynasty. The Almoravids were supplanted after eighty years of rule by the armies of Abd el-Mumen, who took Marrakesh by storm in 1147, and established the Almohad dynasty. Between 1184 and 1198 the third Almohad Sultan, Yacoub el-Mansour, erected the mosque and tower of the Koutobia, which dominates the *medina* to this day. At the same time he built the famous Giralda at Seville and the incomplete 'Tower of Hassan' at Rabat.

After the fall of the Almohads at the end of the thirteenth century Marrakesh waned in importance, and did not come into its own until the Saadian Sultan, Abou Abbas Ahmed el-Mansour made it his principal capital after the conquest of Timbuctoo in 1591. It was, perhaps, during the reign of 'Abou the Golden' that the city reached its zenith. Gold and ivory and slaves poured in from subject kingdoms across the Sahara. Marrakesh grew in wealth and influence. Its coinage circulated in Europe, proclaiming the riches of the Moroccan Empire.

Since that time it has remained the most important city in southern Morocco and the centre of trade with the Sahara and points south. Even now, in spite of competition from the internal combustion engine, more than 20,000 camels cross the desert each year to bring merchandise to the city. Its markets are famous throughout the world, not only for the variety of goods on sale (one can buy anything from an aphrodisiac to a motor-car), but also for its astonishing collection of the races and colours of men. There are Arabs with djellabahs of white, Berbers from the mountains in their blue cloaks, black-capped Jews, dark *Haratin* from the Draa Valley, Sudanese negroes, French soldiers and dishevelled *colons*.

The social centre of the *medina* is a huge open square, the Djemaa el Fna, or 'Concourse of Sinners'. No doubt the name is as appropriate today as it was in the past, when the Sultans used to display in the square the severed heads of criminals and rebels. In normal times it is crowded with little stalls, housing traders of all kinds—vendors of spices and herbs, of bread and fruit and meat; medicine men, barbers, confidence tricksters, letter-writers, story-tellers, snake-charmers, singers, dancers, pimps; catering within the compass of a few acres for every human appetite. But on the occasion of our visit it was almost completely deserted. The city had not yet recovered from the disturbances of the previous day.

In the Djemaa el Fna we were to pick up Humphrey and M'Barek, who were due back from Beni Mellal. We had arranged to meet them at the Café de France, where we waited on the famous roof garden, looking out over the city. Beyond the roofs and minarets we could see the green belt of palms, and further still the shimmering Haouz Plain. Faintly, in the far distance, rose the great peaks of the Atlas. Humphrey and M'Barek duly arrived, but they had not succeeded in finding the camera, and my suspicions of the *ancien militaire* hardened.

Our first call that day was to the office of the Bureau du Contrôle Civil, a branch of the French Government which was responsible for the administration of Morocco north of the Atlas. Its headquarters, a building which was once the palace of a minor nobleman, lay in the *medina*. As we approached it we saw many little groups of white-robed men, chatting together at street corners or in doorways. Their rifles and wooden clubs showed them to be *mohasnis*, soldiers of the Pasha, ready to subdue any disturbance.

At the Contrôle Civil we met Lieutenant G., a charming Marseillais who spoke fluent English. We told him of our desire to set up camp in the mountains, and he did not foresee any difficulties. The Berbers, he said, were friendly to Europeans, and they had been little influenced by the French administration.

The Atlas mountains have long acted as a barrier against Morocco's invaders. Carthaginians, Romans, Vandals, Arabs, Portuguese and Spaniards have all to some extent controlled southern Morocco. But none of them ever secured more than a foothold in the Atlas. It was left to the French, under Marshal Lyautey, finally to subjugate the mountain tribes. It was a hard fight, and the conquest of southern Morocco was not complete until 1934.

The French success was facilitated by the help of the tribal chieftain, Si Hadj Thami el-Glaoui, who became Pasha of Marrakesh and one of the richest men in the world. At the time of our visit he was still a power to be reckoned with, for he held sway over more than a million people and controlled most of southern Morocco. The Pasha's forbears owed their power to the fact that they were chiefs of the *kasbah* (castle) of Telouet, which stood guard over the ancient caravan route from

Marrakesh to the south. But the truly widespread influence of the Glaoui family dated only from the beginning of this century, having reached its zenith after the arrival of the French in 1912. The French have supported the Pasha, not only because of his help during the 'Wars of Pacification', but also because it was in their interest to maintain a strong Government in southern Morocco; a Government which was favourably disposed towards them.

Thami el-Glaoui showed promise of his great political astuteness at an early age. Joseph Thomson, who was the first European to reach Telouet, described the young el-Glaoui, in 1889, as 'a boy of some fifteen years . . . who had an incredible amount of precocious knowledge'. The family's fortunes improved greatly at the end of the nineteenth century when one of his brothers was appointed Grand Vizier to the Sultan; and relations with the Central Government were further improved when el-Glaoui married the daughter of a later Grand Vizier. With the help of both the Sultan and the French, and with his continually increasing wealth, he was able to extend his empires to cover a vast area of southern Morocco, and he became known as 'le Grand Seigneur de l'Atlas', or 'The Sultan of the South'. In these territories his word was law.

I told Lieutenant G., that we had a letter of introduction to the Pasha from Mr Freese-Pennyfather, and that we would very much like to arrange an audience.

'I am very sorry,' he said, 'but he is at the moment in Casablanca.'

'Could we see one of his sons?'

'Perhaps so. . . . I will telephone the Palace. If you call upon me tomorrow I will let you know whether it can be arranged. Si Abd Sadek is in Marrakesh. He is, as you know, one of the most influential of the Pasha's sons. A letter of recommendation from him could be very useful to you.'

After our visit to the Contrôle Civil, we left M'Barek in the *medina* and arranged to collect him later in the evening. We returned to the *gueliz*.

Another person to whom we had an introduction in Marrakesh was General Brissaud-Desmaillet, who was in command of the city garrisons. He very kindly invited us to his home for drinks in the late afternoon. We were received by his wife who entertained us most hospitably until the later arrival of the General, who had come straight from a conference between the Resident and el-Glaoui. I remembered

Lieutenant G.'s information that el-Glaoui was in Casablanca. General Brissaud-Desmaillet had been present at the departure of the Resident from Marrakesh at 6.30 p.m., whereas according to the newspapers he had left in the morning. There were even photographs of his departure. It was clear that extensive precautions were being taken.

The General was horrified to hear of our night spent in the Palmeries, which were dangerous, since they were the haunt of terrorist bands. Perhaps we had more need to be grateful to our nocturnal visitors than we had imagined. Madame kindly insisted that we spend the following night at their home. There, we would be much better defended. Twelve soldiers were stationed on the roof. We accepted, pleased at the prospect of having a roof and twelve soldiers over our heads, and prepared to collect M'Barek from the *medina*. The General said, at first, that he would not hear of our going in after dark without a military escort, but eventually he allowed us to do so, having made certain over the telephone that the city was calm. We had no trouble in extracting M'Barek.

The following morning we returned to the Contrôle Civil for another interview with Lieutenant G. He had arranged for an audience with Si Abd Sadek, and upon our arrival he telephoned to the Palace. This was situated on the opposite side of the *medina* from the Contrôle Civil. A taxi deposited us outside its iron-studded gates. The street was full of the Pasha's soldiers, and many of them were armed with rifles.

We approached the gatekeeper and presented our letter of introduction, telling him that we were expected; but in spite of all our pleas, protests and threats he refused to allow us in. We persisted until he drew back the bolt of his rifle and slid a cartridge into the breech. We returned post-haste to the Contrôle Civil.

Lieutenant G. was apologetic and spent a considerable time at the telephone. Our second assault on the Palace was more successful. The gatekeeper grinned and let us pass. We were shown through a series of white-washed courts, and passing under a pointed archway came into a luxuriant walled garden, in which fountains were playing. The central feature of the garden was an enormous colonnaded pavilion, and on its tiled forecourt were scattered a number of cane chairs. We sat down to await Si Sadek. Looking about me, I decided that the Palace was a little too good to be true. It resembled a Hollywood film director's idea of what should be the home of an Eastern potentate. We later discovered that it had, in fact, been built quite recently.

We had been waiting for about half an hour when a secretary

appeared to tell us that Si Abd Sadek had left Marrakesh and would not return for several days. We went home defeated, but we had learned to be suspicious of information about the movements of important Moroccans. Humphrey and Peter decided to make a further attempt at Si Sadek's private house in the evening. Meanwhile, I visited another official of the French administration, who telephoned to the town of Ait Ourir, our next stopping place. He arranged that we should spend the night there at the home of the Contrôleur Civil, M. de la Boissière. Humphrey and Peter returned late from their expedition, but they had good news. By presenting our letter of introduction at Si Sadek's home, they had finally managed to run him to earth, and he had consented to an interview on the following day. A certain tenacity of purpose was clearly necessary in Moroccan affairs.

Thus it was that Colin, John and I set off with M'Barek to Ait Ourir while Humphrey and Peter stayed in Marrakesh. The countryside between Marrakesh and Ait Ourir was flat and uninteresting semi-desert; there were scattered plantations of palms and occasionally a French farm with carefully irrigated fields. In this type of country, just outside Marrakesh, is found the 'Golf du Pasha', a beautifully laid out eighteen-hole golf course, maintained at enormous expense in perfect condition for the entertainment of el-Glaoui and his guests!

At the French post at Ait Ourir we were greeted cordially by M. de la Boissière, who allowed us to set up camp in his garden, and then invited us to his home for a whisky and soda. He talked of his job as Contrôleur Civil, about which he was clearly an enthusiast. His establishment was a model of efficiency and we noticed that the villagers saluted him with respect. He showed, however, a certain restraint in the company of M'Barek. We felt that perhaps he did not understand our acceptance of a Berber as an equal member of the party. He was enormously proud of his admirable garden, in which we found every conceivable variety of fruit and vegetable, both European and tropical. Cool avenues of palms shaded its walks, and it even boasted a finely cut lawn, a remarkable achievement in the Moroccan climate. It was, too, a splendid place for collecting animals, and I spent a profitable evening chasing butterflies among the flower-beds and catching the small turtles which swam in the irrigation ditches.

The next morning we were awakened by M. de la Boissière in person, very kindly bringing us supplies for breakfast. I spent the first part of the morning digging for earthworms with the help of an enthusiastic squad of gardeners. At about midday Peter and Humphrey arrived from Marrakesh, accompanied by a villainous-looking Berber. He was a *mohasni* in the service of the Pasha, and his name was Abdullah. Si Abd Sadek had been very sympathetic towards our plans, had given us a letter to his *khalifa* at Telouet, and had sent Abdullah to accompany us as our guide and guard. Abdullah had served in the *goums* and spoke a little French. We came to appreciate his talent for making himself, and us, comfortable in unlikely places. He was also very accomplished at intimidating unco-operative officials.

We were now approaching the last stage of our journey. We planned to establish a base camp at the village of Taddert, which was high in the mountains on the road from Ait Ourir to the south. M. de la Boissière arranged that his Adjutant should accompany us to help in our dealing with the Sheikh of Taddert. The Adjutant had a luxurious Studebaker, and Humphrey and I went with him, while the others followed in the truck. This, I felt, was the way in which an expedition should travel—in a comfortable family saloon! The road first crossed flat country, similar to that over which we had passed the previous day, but soon we reached the foothills of the Atlas. The road, which was built during the 'Wars of Pacification' to carry supplies to French troops, climbed the dry hillsides in a series of alarming loops. The Adjutant was an enthusiastic driver, and succeeded in frightening me severely before I realized how well he knew the road. From time to time we passed small villages of flat-roofed stone houses, piled one upon the other like the layers of a wasps' nest. Near each village there was a patch of small terraced fields, carefully irrigated from little mountain streams. The slopes became more and more precipitous. The road curved round them and we could look down over its edge into valleys hundreds of feet below. As we climbed higher we came into the region of greater rainfall, and here the mountain sides were sparsely covered with stunted oaks and junipers, although there were still many areas completely bare of vegetation. We were coming to the highest part of the range and great peaks towered above us. Some still carried the remains of winter snows. Nevertheless on the road below them the heat was intense.

Taddert was a village much like the others we had passed. It contained only twenty or thirty houses, but it boasted an inn, *L'Auberge des Noyers*, which catered for travellers on the road. At the back of the inn was a small terrace shaded by almond trees, and here the Sheikh awaited us. Colourful carpets had been laid on the ground and we politely removed our shoes before sitting down—with the exception, that is, of the Adjutant.

As is often the habit in Morocco a great deal of time was occupied with mutual introductions. We discovered not only that the Sheikh was well and happy, but also that his wives and children were similarly blessed. We found that his affairs had progressed in a satisfactory fashion. We heard that the crops in the village this year were expected to be large. It is probable that none of this was true, but good manners demanded that it be said.

After a short time two servants brought a brass tray with tea-pot, small glasses, and an urn filled with fresh mint. One of them squatted down to boil water in a kettle over a small charcoal burner. The Sheikh prepared tea. Mint-tea is the Moroccan national drink, consumed in great quantities at every possible occasion. Preparing it is both a ritual and an art, and the greatest compliment a host can pay to his guest is to ask him to make the tea. The first time that this happened to me proved to be embarrassing. The result was almost undrinkable, but of course our host politely praised my skill.

After tea came luncheon. The two servants appeared again with a brass ewer and basin, in which we ceremonially washed our hands. Then a low brass table was brought in and an enormous dish placed in its centre. The removal of its conical cover revealed a steaming stew of mutton, vegetables and spices. We squatted round it in a circle. Custom allowed us to eat with only the first three fingers of the right hand. There is a Moorish saying: 'To eat with one finger is a sign of hatred [and, I might add, considerable dexterity], to eat with two shows pride, to eat with three accords with the *sunna* [the practice of the prophet], to eat with four or five is a sign of gluttony.' We all soon fell into the last category. The Adjutant used *both* hands. The first stew was followed by a second, also of mutton, but prepared in a different way. Then came *kus-kus*. This is millet which has been steamed over a saucepan in which meat is being stewed. It is nearly always the final course of a Moroccan meal. In the eating of *kus-kus*, little balls are formed by a peculiar motion of the half-closed hand. These are then raised to the edge of the fist and dexterously shot into the mouth by the thumb. To do this properly demands considerable practice, and we succeeded in spreading a good deal over the carpet. The meal was rounded off with fruit and another brew of mint-tea.

It was now permissible to discuss business. The Sheikh said that he would arrange for men to guide us to the surrounding villages so that we might select one which would be suitable for our survey. The Adjutant suggested that we study a village near Taddert, so that we could live at the inn. He seemed very keen to persuade us not to set up our camp a great distance from the road. He conveyed his reluctance to the Sheikh, but when we pressed the point he said that he would provide mules to carry our supplies. We parted with expressions of goodwill, and the Adjutant returned to Ait Ourir.

The *patron* of the inn, although clearly at a loss to understand our presence, gave us permission to set up our camp beds on the terrace. It was a pleasant place with a magnificent view across the valley to a small village on the opposite slopes. We sat out in the evening, eating our supper under a trellised vine, watching the moon rise above the peaks, and discussing our plans for the next few days.

Between Taddert and Telouet is the watershed of the Atlas, whose summits catch the rains and snows of winter. Here there are steep valleys, difficult of access, with small communities of Berber tribesmen. We planned to live in one of these communities and to study its tribal organization, agricultural methods and local crafts.

The Berbers have inhabited Morocco, and indeed the whole of North Africa, since very early times. In Marrakesh and the south they far outnumber the Arabs. Since the two races have been intermarrying for more than a thousand years, it is often impossible to tell the racial origin of a particular man or woman. Nevertheless, large numbers of pure Berbers still survive, particularly in remote mountain regions.

In general, the Moroccan Arab is darker than the Berber, with Semitic features, and often a hooked nose. He has a lazier, more easy-going disposition, a penetrating mind, and a great fondness for pre-varication. This last characteristic was famous even in the time of Aesop, during the fifth century B.C. One of the fables attributed to him tells the story that the god Hermes drove across the world with a cart stuffed with falsehoods, wickedness and deceit. He distributed a small part of his load in each country. But when he came to the country of the Arabs the cart suddenly broke in pieces and the inhabitants, thinking that its contents were valuable merchandise, plundered it. There was nothing left for Hermes to carry elsewhere. Aesop sums up his tale by saying: 'The Arabs are the greatest liars and deceivers on earth.' This is, perhaps, an overstatement.

The Berber often has a fairer complexion than many Europeans. His face is short and broad, with high cheekbones and slanting eyes, which give him an almost Mongolian appearance. The Berbers are more down-to-earth than the Arabs, and more reserved. They are usually practical men, clever with their hands, and not much given to intellectual pursuits. They have a higher regard for the truth, and their reputation for honesty is as ancient as that of the Arabs for prevarication. Herodotus writes:

> The Carthaginians also tell us that they trade with a race of men who live in a part of Libya beyond the Pillar of Heracles. On reaching this country, they unload their goods, arranging them tidily along the beach, and then returning to their boats raise smoke. Seeing the smoke, the natives come down to the beach, place on the ground a certain quantity of gold in exchange for the goods, and go off again to a distance. The Carthaginians then come ashore and take a look at the gold; and if they think it represents a fair price for their wares, they collect it and go away; if, on the other hand, it seems too little they go back aboard and wait, and the natives come and add to the gold until they are satisfied. There is perfect honesty on both sides; the Carthaginians never touch the gold until it equals in value what they have offered for sale, and the natives never touch the goods until the gold has been taken away.

It is possible, however, that this story refers to the Negroes of the Sudan.

The origin of the Berber race is a mystery. One theory suggests that they are a Celtic-Iberian mixture and that they migrated from Spain many thousands of years ago. Comparisons have been drawn, none too successfully, between their language and Welsh. Recent studies have shown that in the frequency of some of their blood groups they strongly resemble the Basques of northern Spain, whom anthropologists believe to be survivors of a race which formerly populated much of Europe.

Another theory suggests that the Berbers spring from Phoenicians who migrated from the Levant. There is a tradition that they are descended from Canaanites forced out of Palestine by the armies of Joshua. It seems likely, at any rate, that the Berbers are not of African origin, although they have lived in the region of the Sahara for a very long time.

The word 'Berber' may be derived from the Greek βάρβαροι, but

E

the tribal titles 'Barabara' and 'Beraberata' appear in Egyptian inscriptions of 1700 and 1300 B.C. The Berbers were known to the Egyptians as the 'Lebu' (Libyans), and to the Romans as 'Numidae' (English, 'nomad'), 'Gaetuli' (from the name 'Gued'oula'—the great Berber tribe) and 'Mauri' (from the Hebrew 'Mahur'—western). On the monuments of Egypt their ancestors are depicted with the comparatively blond features which many of them still display.

Because of intermarriage it is difficult to say how many there are of Berber race, but the language is spoken by some five million people, not only in Morocco but also in Algeria, Tunisia and in great stretches of the Sahara. There are many dialects, of which two are spoken in Morocco: Tamazirt in the north-east, and Tachelhait in the region of Marrakesh and the south-west. These two dialects are about as different as broad Scots and Devonian. The language has little or no resemblance to Arabic or to any African tongue. Its constructions are peculiar. Plurals, for instance, are often derived by shortening the first syllable of a word and adding *en* at the end, as with the English word *child*. The Berber *afus* (hand) has the plural *ifassen*. A masculine noun is often made feminine by adding *t* (or *th*) at the beginning and the end. For example, the word for mule, *aseroun*, is made feminine as *thaserount*. The feminine plural becomes *thiseroyathin*. There are a very few words which seem to have been derived from Latin or Greek. *Anjlus* (child) certainly bears a strong resemblance to the Latin *angelus* or the Greek ἄγγελος, and *afithal* (rest house) seems similar to the Latin *hospita* and the English *hospital*.

No modern Berber dialect is written except that of the Touareg, whose strange rectilinear inscriptions decorate so many stony outcrops in the Sahara. Recently a number of Berber writings of about two thousand years ago have been excavated at sites along the North African coast. These bear a very close resemblance to the Touareg inscriptions of today.

Before the Arab invasions of the seventh century, most of the Berbers practised a primitive animistic form of religion, although some, like St Augustine, were Christians. When, however, the Arabs finally conquered Morocco, the tribes were gradually converted to Islam. But pockets of resistance remained in the mountains, and even today the mountain tribes show traces of ancient animistic beliefs. The worship of saints and their relics is stronger here than elsewhere in Islam, and in some parts propitiatory offerings are placed before certain trees, rocks, or springs which are supposed to be holy or to be inhabited by spirits.

*   *   *   *

We hoped to discover a village which was far enough from the road to be unaffected by the influences of French civilization. We did not share the Adjutant's enthusiasm for Taddert. It was a picturesque place, but many of its inhabitants had forsaken their traditional ways to ape the behaviour of Europeans. We found them hanging about the inn, dressed in cheap European clothes, drinking Pepsi-Cola or Coca-Cola, ever willing to sponge upon the visitor.

The Adjutant had said, 'In Taddert you can be comfortable. Why should you wish to trouble yourselves by camping in the mountains?' He did not understand that we wished to study the tribesmen in their own environment, not in the artificial circumstances of a halting-place on the motor road. Taddert was an arid place, and had few fields or pastures. But we wanted to study a village that was predominantly agricultural—with good supplies of water and with fertile earth. The village must also be small, so that we could conveniently survey the utilization of its lands.

The map showed, about three miles to the north of Taddert, a place called Tamguemguemt, which might be suitable. We decided to start the search on the morrow.

The Sheikh himself went with us to Tamguemguemt. (Its name, we found, was pronounced 'Tamagimagimt'.) Our path left the road a short distance out of Taddert as we climbed up a dry stream bed. The Sheikh rode a splendid mule; the rest of us walked. Abdullah strode ahead, and the long curved dagger which was slung from his shoulder glinted in the sun.

From time to time Colin and I stopped to collect animals. We found enormous fat black crickets about three inches long crawling on the dry cushion plants, and innumerable grasshoppers. The catching of grasshoppers is a difficult sport. These insects are very quick of eye and they will leap out of range at the sweep of a butterfly net. But unfortunately for them, they are limited by their anatomy; they have to jump in the direction in which they are pointing. It is possible to catch them by sweeping the butterfly net in front of them, so that they jump into it. Colin and I wasted a lot of time before we discovered this.

A little further on we found a chameleon wandering along the path. It was captured and housed in Colin's pocket.

The vegetation became sparser as we climbed the stream-bed, and the black basaltic rocks reflected the heat of the sun. We were becoming tired, and the Sheikh allowed me to try my hand at riding his mule. The animal clearly understood that its rider was inexperienced, and behaved as mules are popularly supposed to do. It stopped and refused to budge. The Sheikh cut a stick and sharpened it to a fine point. He told me to encourage the beast by prodding it on the shoulder. I duly prodded gently, not wishing to injure the animal, but this produced no response at all. Finally in irritation I gave it a hard jab. The mule bolted, and I struggled to stay on its back as we raced crazily down the path. Mercifully it soon became tired, and stopped.

I never mastered the art of mulemanship; my progress was always in fits and starts. Nevertheless the animals were remarkably sure-footed on difficult paths, and it was possible to ride them in places where a man would hesitate to walk. The tribesmen, when climbing steep hills, grasp the mule's tail, so that it pulls them along. Strangely enough the animals seem not to resent this, for I did not hear of anyone being kicked.

We found the Moroccan saddle difficult. It consists of a very thickly woven blanket which is thrown over the animal's back and secured with strings under its belly. The front part of the blanket has pockets at each corner which accommodate the rider's toes and serve as stirrups. The Berbers on the whole are short men, and I found that when my feet were in the stirrups my knees projected above the animal's back. It was a very uncomfortable mode of transport.

Half an hour's journey brought us to Tamguemguemt, a small village in a steep valley between slopes of bare cinder-like scree. Its few stone houses straggled alongside a sluggish stream. It must have been a hard place to live, and the difficult conditions seemed to be reflected in the behaviour of its people. They were surly, and received us with ill grace. They seemed interested only in the possibilities of extracting our money. We felt that we were still too near the road and other 'civilizing' influences. The Sheikh, however, was very keen that we should study Tamguemguemt. He extolled its many virtues, and led us to the top of a nearby hill so that we could see it to the best advantage. Its aspect certainly improved with distance, and from our point of vantage it was almost possible to like the place. Huge mountain peaks towered around it, and the village seemed pathetically insignificant amongst them. A short distance below us, on an outcrop of rock, there was a walled area where men were winnowing grain. They threw great yellow clouds of it up into the evening breeze, letting the wind carry away the chaff. Below them by the stream women were tending a few emaciated cows.

We resisted the blandishments of the Sheikh, and returned home to search the map for another village. There was one called Tafraoute which looked promising, and the Sheikh said he would provide us with someone to lead us there on the following day.

The guide, whose name was Mohammed, arrived punctually at about eight o'clock in the morning. The path again lay through Tamguemguemt, but this time we went beyond it. Above the village there were magnificent views across the mountains. It was very hot, and we were exhausted when finally we arrived at Tafraoute. The villagers refreshed us with mint-tea, served in the shade of an enormous oak. While sitting on the cool grass we tried to work out our position from the map. It was some time before we discovered that we were not in the village of our choice. There were, it seems, two Tafraoutes, one on each side of a large mountain, and we were in the wrong one. We later learned to view our maps with great suspicion. One of them reproduced a single river twice. According to this map the two 'rivers' were over ten miles apart.

On the way home John lagged behind, digging up plants, and when we reached Tamguemguemt he was nowhere to be seen. Abdullah became very agitated; he felt responsible for our safety. It was not wise for a single person to wander in the mountains, he said; the people were all villains. They would undoubtedly slay John and rob him and then the Pasha would have Abdullah shot.

It was very convincing, and we became worried about John's safety. But eventually he wandered in, unrobbed, unslain, and unrepentant.

This provoked a quarrel. I asked him not to go off alone. He accused me of being an 'old woman'.

The next day, Humphrey, John and Peter departed to look for the other Tafraoute. Colin and I occupied ourselves collecting insects on the slopes around Taddert. It was tiring work, and we spent most of the afternoon resting in the bar of the *auberge* and talking to the *patron* and his customers. The inn catered mainly for drivers of the trucks which carried supplies to the French posts in the south. Occasionally, too, came men who had driven across the Sahara from the Sudan. The truck-drivers would appear only briefly, to drink wine or an *apéritif*, or to gulp down a quick meal. There were one or two residents, however, who stayed at the inn to avoid the summer heat. One of them was a fat Frenchman, owner of a small transport company in the north, on holiday with his wife and child. He amused himself in the afternoons with a rifle, shooting frogs in the stream. He did not eat them; it was, he said, 'for the sport'.

The *patron* had been a member of the Foreign Legion during the wars in the 1920s and 30s. Foreseeing the necessity for a halting place on the road, he had built the inn when he retired. Now an old man, he lived there with his friends and occasional helpers.

The fare at the inn was simple, but expensive. Almost everything had to be transported from Marrakesh, but the *patron* had some profitable arrangements with truck-drivers who brought him supplies.

The bar was a dark place. It had grimy painted walls, decorated with antique French advertisements, and even grimier marble-topped tables. But one could obtain a surprising variety of goods, even including brands of British and American cigarettes and soft drinks.

There is an anecdote—I do not know the truth of it—about the competition between local salesmen of two popular kinds of soft drink. One, it is said, which was first upon the scene, somehow gained the reputation for being a very efficient aphrodisiac. Moroccans are much concerned about their virility, and sales boomed. However, when the manufacturers of the other drink opened up an agency in Morocco, another rumour circulated: that the first contained pig's blood. Pig is abhorrent to any good Muslim, and the second drink gained in popularity. These rumours of course were patently untrue, and both beverages now have a large sale in Morocco.

Humphrey, Peter and John returned in the evening from their visit to the second Tafraoute. They were enthusiastic, and described it as a sort of Shangri-La.

Their path had led north from Taddert along the tarmac motor road before they turned east to descend into the river-bed. The party wound its way through tamarisk bushes, crossed the river at a ford, and followed the course of one of its tributaries. The stream-bed was filled with a jumble of boulders, its sides were bare rocky scree. About two miles along the path they came to a single house which stood on a spur of rock jutting out into the valley. Below it there were a few terraced fields. It was the last inhabited dwelling in what had once been a prosperous village. The village had been destroyed during tribal wars, and a single family remained, eking out a miserable and solitary existence. The head of the family invited them in and gave them buttermilk in an earthenware pot, which was passed round from mouth to mouth. They drank carefully, avoiding the scum of dirt which floated on its surface.

At the top of the valley the path climbed steeply through juniper scrub, doubling monotonously back and forth. Finally it breasted a pass, and the travellers saw the valley of the Ait Rbaa spread out thousands of feet below them. After the stark countryside through which they had passed, it was good to see the green fields, the villages, and the plantations of walnut-trees that made islands of shade in the bright sun. To the south the valley was dominated by multiple summits of Djebel Tistouit, and the col that led to Telouet. In the north, the stream meandered—a green ribbon between bleak buttresses of rock.

There were men and women working in the fields as they came down into the valley. Men were shouting to scare the birds from their crops, others were thinning out the maize, and there were women washing clothes in the stream. They had seen this microcosmic picture of the village undisturbed, from far up the mountain side, but then, as they drew nearer, they realized suddenly that there was not a man or woman to be seen. Mohammed became disturbed, and they halted. One by one women appeared on the roof-tops to spy out their movements. The village had followed its customs, developed at the time of tribal warfare, when only the women were safe from the invader. It was as if it had gone into a state of siege. Humphrey, Peter and John were the enemy, to be watched and guarded against until their purpose was made clear. They sent Mohammed and Abdullah, to explain their visit, to the Sheikh who lived in the furthest of the six villages of the valley.

They had been waiting an hour, when a man came running, his *djellaba* hitched up above his knees, to call them to the Sheikh.

The Sheikh, a stout man with a scar beneath his left eye, greeted them formally outside his house. He preceded them into a long austere whitewashed room, in which the only decoration was a single print of the prophet's tomb. From the windows they could look down over the shambles of roof-tops and alleyways which made up the village, to walnut-trees and the stream that ran down the narrow valley. Several dignified elders followed them into the room and sat about the walls. There was a tense silence. A young man began to make tea over a brazier, and another waved a fan to keep away the flies. Frenchmen came seldom to the valley, they said, and Englishmen they had never seen. So far as their dignified reserve allowed it, they were intrigued.

Peter, Humphrey and John were impressed by the isolation of this community and by the bearing of its people, so different from the men who hung about the *cantine*. They were determined that we should set up camp in the Ait Rbaa, and infected Colin and me with their enthusiasm for the valley, which they described as 'verdant'.

It is interesting to observe how greatly a person's impressions of a place depend upon previous circumstances. The first European to visit the region, Joseph Thomson, passed through the Ait Rbaa on his way to Telouet. He reached the valley only after enormous difficulties, and these perhaps coloured his description.

> Yet the glen was not wholly desolate, for even here the hardy mountaineers, braving all the terrors of winter and the arid heats of summer, had established themselves, and forced from the flinty bosom of mother earth the wherewithal to eke out an existence. . . . Something of the stern, sad aspect of the mountains was reflected too in the people themselves. Folded in their black goats' hair *kanif*, or cloak, with conical cowl drawn over their heads, they sat like inanimate objects on house-top or boulder watching our passing with stern yet somewhat lacklustre eyes, their wrinkled and weather-beaten faces, spare forms, and small stature telling plainly of the hard battle they had to fight with the forces of Nature arrayed against them. . . . The mountains circled round this crater-like depression in unbroken frowning precipices. . . . In this dreary solitude stood the village of Titula . . . a more unpromising region for plant-collecting I could not have selected. What was lacking in numbers, variety and scientific value, was made up in sentimental interest, however.

John later collected over five hundred species of plant in the region.

That evening we paid a visit to the Sheikh of Taddert, who promised us twenty mules so that we might leave for the Ait Rbaa on the following day. We worked late into the night unloading our boxes from the truck and arranging the supplies in mule-loads. The *patron* gave us permission to leave 'Tartarin' at the *auberge*.

We awoke early, hoping to find our caravan of mules at the door, but the village was deserted. We searched for the Sheikh and discovered that he had left for a conference with the Pasha in Marrakesh. We were told that there were no mules available. The aerial railway which carried manganese ore across the mountains had broken down and the mining company had commandeered all local mules. The Sheikh must have known this when he offered them to us.

Two days later there were still no mules. 'Perhaps there will be some tomorrow, *insha' Allah*, if God wills.'

'*Insha' Allah.*'

Insha' Allah was a popular expression. Conversation was full of it, and in some way it represented the Moroccan's humility before the force of circumstances, his realization of the fallibility of man.

'Tomorrow,' he would say, 'I will visit you, *insha'Allah*.'

Three days later he would come, offering no explanation for the delay. It was merely that circumstances had prevented him. One could not, after all, strive successfully against the forces of nature or the will of God.

To a European trying to organize his programme according to a time-table, their attitude seemed to be one of calculated cussedness. But this was not so. They behaved in this way with each other, and did not see it as being likely to cause offence. It annoyed us at first, but we became resigned to it, and very soon we began to use the phrase ourselves, albeit somewhat wryly.

In the afternoon we were sitting despondently at the bar discussing alternative means of transport, when a visitor came in. In excruciatingly bad French, he demanded a drink. He was elegantly dressed in a sports coat and trousers, but wore peculiar cotton shoes of a type that I had not seen. His face was thin and heavily tanned. I decided that he was a Scandinavian, but Peter was doubtful. We were arguing the point hotly in English when he turned and introduced himself.

'Are you the people from Oxford?' he asked. Embarrassed, we nodded assent.

'I'm Wilfred Thesiger. I heard about you from the Consulate at Rabat.'

Mr Thesiger was a traveller of some renown. On coming down from Magdalen before the war he immediately set off to walk, with no European companions, across the country of the Danakils in Abyssinia. The Danakils were noted for their habit of murdering visitors, but Thesiger succeeded where others had failed. Since that time he had led a nomadic existence in remote parts of the world, visiting the interior of the Sahara, crossing the Empty Quarter of Arabia by camel, and staying for five years with the marshmen of southern Iraq. He had come to Taddert with the intention of walking across the spine of the Atlas to Azrou in eastern Morocco, a journey of some 300 miles. He carried only a small suitcase.

I remembered that on the ferry to Tangier I had made a bet with Colin that we would meet, in some remote part of Morocco, at least one Oxford man. I collected my bet.

Thesiger joined us in our 'camp' on the terrace. He told us that he had obtained his curious shoes in Kurdistan, and we spent an enjoyable evening listening to hair-raising tales of adventure. We discussed our inability to get mules in Taddert, and he suggested that we should all go to Telouet, where perhaps our letters of introduction might help us to obtain the necessary animals. We could not leave immediately, because the next day was a religious festival.

Our conversation was interrupted by the appearance of a young man, who sported a sweater of startling hue. He addressed us.

'You collect animals? I got nice bird. Very nice. You like? I give him to you. I like English. Speak English good. Work with Americans. Americans, English, same-same thing, yes?' Many Moroccans, when speaking pidgin English, will say: 'same-same' rather than 'same'. The Arabic word is *kif-kif*.

We accepted the bird with thanks. He was a splendid creature about ten inches long, pale azure blue with a bright chestnut back. He was one of the rollers, which catch flying insects on the wing, and we named him 'Clarence'. A well-behaved bird, he would sit about peacefully, only occasionally giving a crow-like 'caw'.

The following day was *Aid el Kebir* (The Great Feast) which is one of the major celebrations in the Mohammedan calendar. On this day the head of each family sacrifices a number of sheep. The animals are held facing in the direction of Mecca, and then their throats are cut. The bodies of these sheep are supposed to be very potent in *baraka* (blessing, or good luck) and their skulls may be put under trees to protect domestic animals from accident. The choicer parts of their anatomy are dried, to be eaten on special occasions. It has been estimated that in Morocco alone more than a million sheep are slaughtered at this time every year. *Aid el Kebir* is also the occasion for excesses of religious fervour (often taking the form of the elimination of infidels), and the French authorities had advised us to be circumspect during the festivities. They did say, however, that 'unpleasant events' were unlikely to occur in the mountains. In Taddert the first part of the celebration was a meeting in the mosque, attended by the men of the village, who wore their best white robes for the occasion. The Taddert mosque, like so many in the smaller settlements, was a low stone-and-mud building virtually indistinguishable from the houses.

After the ceremony the men walked in solemn procession along the road, singing their strange traditional chants. The singers were divided into groups, and each would begin or end a fragment of the song, seemingly at random. But I soon realized that, although the fragments might in themselves be meaningless, yet they were contributing to the drama of the whole. Human voices were serving as instruments in an orchestra to create an effect far more impressive than any simple melody. There was a heightened emotion in the swelling voices which conveyed their rejoicing in the occasion, and their confidence in the Muslim faith.

The fat hunter of frogs came to the ceremony dressed in shorts. He must have known that they are an abomination to the Moors. He stood in front of the procession, ostentatiously taking photographs, until it had nearly reached him, when he condescended to move aside. I felt that they showed great forbearance in not turning *him* to Mecca, and cutting his throat.

The afternoon was given over to feasting, and we decided, feeling rather out of things, to investigate the source of a waterfall which we could see high on a mountain above the village.

We drove the truck towards the top of the pass. The slopes here were even steeper than before, and the road was constructed cleverly, doubling back upon itself every few hundred yards, and in places appearing even to overhang great precipices. There was no fence along the outside edge, so that the drive was sometimes alarming. We parked the truck near the top of the pass, and climbed a gentle grassy slope which led to the summit of Djebel bou Ourioul, the 'Mountain of the Donkey'. At about 9,000 feet we found the source of the waterfall. It was an irrigation ditch which carried the stream to the edge of a cliff. We sat down to rest on its bank, and watched hawks soaring out over the valleys. There were small kites, Egyptian vultures, and huge Lammergeyers with a wing-span of seven feet.

The irrigation ditch indicated the work of man. We followed it, to find a green valley hidden among the peaks. There were lush meadows, cows grazing upon them, and a few stone huts roofed with juniper boughs. At the upper end of the valley were sharp pinnacles of rock. The scene reminded me of the Austrian Tyrol. A man came out of one of the huts and hailed us, inviting us to cross the stream and accept his hospitality. We squatted in the darkness of his house and sipped butter-milk, while he roasted liver over a charcoal fire.

He seemed pleased to see us, and perhaps his valley, in spite of its beauty, was a lonely place. Thanking him for his kindness, we departed and followed a stream which ran back towards the road. About a mile further on, there was another settlement. The people here were more enterprising, perhaps because they were nearer civilization. A woman came out and offered to sell us eggs. Having succeeded in doing so, she hinted that her husband was away and that she was lonely. Would we not like to stay the night? Her daughter was also available. Morality apart, we found neither of them particularly attractive. We continued on our way.

We returned to the truck to find John once again missing. We waited for him, becoming more and more worried. After about three-quarters of an hour he limped in, liberally spattered with blood. He had wandered off by himself to collect plants, and he had dropped his ice-axe over a cliff. Being a keen mountaineer he decided to climb down the cliff-face; but the rock was rotten and it broke away in his hands, and he fell thirty feet. He was lucky to get away with only minor lacerations and a cracked elbow. We bundled him off to Marrakesh hospital, and he did not return for two weeks.

The next day we filled up with petrol at the *auberge* and set off to Telouet. The first part of our journey was the same as on the previous day, but later we crossed, at a height of over 7,000 feet, the summit of the Tizi-n-Tishka Pass, where there is a stone memorial commemorating the engineers who built the road. The south side of the mountains is surprisingly different from the north. The air coming in from the Atlantic deposits most of its water on the northern slopes. By the time it passes over the southern ones there is little left. Consequently these slopes are even drier and more bare. There are, however, a few scattered juniper bushes. The geology also changes, and the rocks in the south tend to be yellow instead of black. They contain a higher proportion of clay, so that although the countryside is generally drier, the soil, where water does occur, retains it more effectively and vegetation is more luxuriant. A few miles beyond the top of the pass the track branches left across the dry plateau. As the truck rumbled along it we saw gangs of workmen laying down tarmac on the road. In one place there was even a steam-roller puffing slowly across the desert. It was an incongruous sight, but it spoke much for the enterprise of el-Glaoui. From time to time we crossed dried-up river-beds spanned by neat concrete bridges. We passed several mud-brick villages, each surrounded by its own plantations of palms and olives. We had been travelling for ten miles before we first sighted the *kasbah*.

Telouet has been described as the most beautiful castle in Morocco. It is certainly an impressive sight, lying as it does in the centre of a vast red dust-bowl enclosed by bleak mountains. After so many miles of uninterrupted redness, its whitewashed walls are dazzling to the eye.

The road in its later stages was already surfaced with tar. We passed the prosperous village of Telouet. The houses looked well kept; many of them even had window-boxes with gay flowers growing in them. Here again one sensed the activities of an organizing power. There was none of the picturesque squalor which we had come to associate with the usual Atlas settlements.

Finally we came to the blank walls of the *kasbah*, punctured only by a pair of heavy wooden gates. We banged upon them, and eventually a tribesman answered our call. But he could not receive us, since the Khalifa was away in a neighbouring village. We were forced to wait for most of the afternoon in the shade of some nearby olive trees.

Clarence was becoming restive in the back of the truck, so we brought him out and tied him to a convenient branch. The chameleon, now known as George, stayed happily in the cool dark interior of the pressure cooker.

The Khalifa at last arrived in a Standard Vanguard, and we followed him through the gates into the *kasbah*. Inside, the road continued for some distance between high walls, through two further gates, before it finally debouched into a walled courtyard.

It was here that the Khalifa received us. He sat cross-legged on a carpeted ledge, surrounded by white-robed elders, and greeted us gravely, accepting our proffered letter. He passed it to his *taleb*—an official versed in the arts of reading and writing. The Khalifa was a squat man in a spotless blue *djellaba*, and he regarded us coldly while the letter was being read.

It was clear that he was a person of some importance in Telouet, since from time to time a tribesman would approach, bow, kiss his hand, and then depart without a word having been spoken. He received this homage with royal dignity. The courtyard was busy. Women were driving cattle across it to an arched doorway on the other side, mules were being unloaded, and the Khalifa's Vanguard was being backed into a rococo garage. Some of the Pasha's long-limbed lean Saluki hunting dogs lay panting in the sun.

The *taleb* droned on. When he had finished, the Khalifa permitted himself a smile and said, briefly and to the point: 'You are welcome to our hospitality. The mules will be ready tomorrow. Please go in.' He motioned to a black servant, who led us through a pointed archway. We found ourselves in another, smaller, courtyard, and on climbing some wooden steps entered a whitewashed room which was furnished with rich carpets and cushions. Leaving our shoes at the door, we arranged ourselves on the cushions and waited.

The windows looked out into a walled area where women were winnowing grain in the evening wind. A donkey squealed in the distance. As the sun set we heard the sing-song cry of the *muezzin* on the mosque calling the people to prayer. After a short time two servants brought in a silver tray, teapot and kettle, and began to prepare mint-tea.

The recipe for its preparation is a simple one: enough green tea to cover the palm of the hand is placed in the pot, and boiling water is poured over it; the resulting liquid is then tipped away. Fresh mint is trimmed to remove dead leaves and it is put—stalks and all—into the teapot. About a quarter of a pound of sugar is added; more boiling water is poured in and the pot left to stew. It is sampled from time to time until it reaches the right concentration. It is then poured into small glasses—and drunk extremely hot.

At first we found it very difficult to hold the hot glasses, and the tea burnt our mouths. But eventually we developed the proper technique, which involved sucking tea and air at the same time—a proceeding which made an unpleasant noise. This sound came to be associated in our minds with the refreshing taste of mint. It had the same effect upon us as the sound of a bell had on Pavlov's dogs, encouraging salivation.

There are certain observances in the drinking of tea. Before the first sip everyone must devoutly say: '*Bismillah*', 'In the name of God.' In polite company only three glasses are consumed, and when the host offers a fourth, it is the signal for the guests to depart. Among friends, however, the tea-drinking can go on *ad infinitum* (or more correctly, *ad nauseam*). There are many connoisseurs of tea in Morocco, and an expert can tell the difference between all the many varieties of mint. In more sophisticated circles other flavourings may also be added; orange-blossom is particularly popular.

After dinner, which consisted of the usual succession of mutton stews followed by *kus-kus*, we strolled through the courtyards of the *kasbah*. It was a scene straight from the Arabian Nights. In each courtyard there were carpeted ledges on which white-cowled figures lounged, gossiping idly or pulling gently at long hashish pipes. They greeted us solemnly as we passed by. From time to time we could see in through lighted windows to where more men lounged on cushions talking and drinking. There was one element, however, disturbing these pictures of barbaric splendour: the rooms were lit by electric light, generated by an ancient steam engine puffing vigorously in the furthest courtyard. We returned to our room, settled heavily down upon the cushions, and almost immediately fell asleep.

At sunrise we were wakened by the call of the *muezzin*, 'Prayer is better than sleep,' and breakfasted soon after on black coffee spiced with pepper, a sort of doughnut, and wild honey. We received visitors curious to learn of our native country. They were sympathetic when we told them that although it was smaller than Morocco there were many more people.

'The oases must be very crowded,' they said.

At about ten o'clock I suddenly remembered that we had left Clarence tied to his branch outside the gates. I ran out to the olive trees, and found only a broken string and a few feathers scattered upon the ground. I do not know what fate befell him, but I felt very guilty about having left him behind.

We prepared to leave. The time had now come for Abdullah, our guide and friend, to return to his duties in Marrakesh. He had escorted us to the *kasbah*; from now on we would be in the care of the Khalifa's officers. We were sorry to see him go, for in spite of his alarmist tendencies he had served us well and cheerfully. We noticed that even in the stronghold of Telouet he was treated with respect.

At the same time as we left for the Ait Rbaa, Thesiger was due to set off on his walk across the Atlas. I had an idea, which I put to him with some trepidation. Would it be possible, I asked, for one of us to accompany him on his journey? It would be a magnificent opportunity for us to extend the scope of our work. Very kindly he agreed. Since

there were two zoologists in the party, and since Colin had a camera
and colour film, he was delegated to go. Thesiger promised that they
would be back within five weeks.

We spent the morning unloading our equipment from the truck and
packing it on the backs of twenty mules. The caravan made an impressive sight as we left the *kasbah* and toiled across the flat gravel plain to
the north of Telouet.

CHAPTER SIX

The Valley of the Ait Rbaa

They cannot look out far.
They cannot look in deep.
But when was that ever a bar
To any watch they keep?

ROBERT FROST

As the hours wore on and the sun rose to its zenith the caravan continued on its way. The path now ran up steep mountain slopes, stony and hot under foot. As we clambered over the rocks the muleteers began to sing the strange lilting Berber songs—songs which spread out on the noonday air, and like the heat were reflected from the walls of rock. They were still singing as we reached the top of the pass and looked across the bare eroded slopes to the green valley below. Then suddenly, as one man, they became silent. One of them jumped from his mule and shouted out a long prayer of thanksgiving. He picked up a stone and set it upon a high cairn, whose size testified to the faith of others who had passed this way. The cairn signified the place where a holy man was supposed to have prayed; a stone placed on such a pile of rocks is believed to act as a link between the suppliant and the saint. Such beliefs evidently date from before the conversion of the Berbers to Islam, and are derived from the more ancient animistic religion.

The caravan started on its downward journey. Far below we could see two small figures striding down the winding path. They were *mohasni* of the Pasha hurrying on to warn the villages of our coming.

An hour later we reached Anammer, where the Sheikh of the Ait Rbaa has his home. The Sheikh was away, but his brother awaited us as we dismounted from our mules. He led us into the same whitewashed room in which the Sheikh had entertained our first mission. We drank mint-tea, and talked. Conversation seemed to show that the most suitable village in the valley would be Idirh, about two miles to the south.

F

65

With the help of the Sheikh's right-hand man, a small person who flourished a frightening wooden club as a sign of his office, we selected a camp site by the stream below Idirh. When the caravan reached a point about a mile from the camp site the mule-men refused to go down to the stream-bed. They wished to get back to Telouet before nightfall; they had much work, they said, to occupy them at home. They had not been paid by the Khalifa, he had merely ordered them to go with us.

I asked M'Barek to deal with the situation. He spoke to them for a few moments in Arabic, and they immediately continued on their way. I asked him what he had said.

'I just suggested that any man who wished to return home should give me his name. I promised to pass it on to the Khalifa.'

I felt badly that these men had not been paid a fair wage for their work, so I presented each man with a hundred francs (all we could afford), and offered as some recompense to give medical treatment to any who were ill. This was unwise. Everyone immediately developed the most alarming symptoms, and never were there so many sick men gathered together in one party. Muleteers stood about wailing, clutching their heads and looking deathly pale. Some of the acting was magnificent; it was clear that many had missed their vocation. I distributed large quantities of aspirin.

Our camp was under a walnut tree, about 200 feet below the village. We were within ten yards of the stream, but it was obviously unsuitable for drinking, for it seemed to contain every conceivable kind of pollution. We discovered, however, that there was a spring about a mile further upstream in a side-valley, and it was from here that the village got its drinking water. Every day the women brought enormous water-jars from the village and filled them at the spring. We were obliged to do the same with our jerrycans. It was a tiring business.

We had been camped for two days before we received our first visitors. They came in single file down the steep path from the village, their *djellabas* hitched up above their knees. They paused at the edge of the camp.

'Peace be unto you,' they said.

'Unto you be peace.'

'You are well?'

'We are well. Thanks to God.'

Greetings over, we invited them in and they sat hesitantly on the edge of our camp beds. We made tea, and I introduced the members of our party. We asked our guests for their names.

'Mohammed,' said the first.

'Mohammed,' said the second.

'Mohammed,' said the third.

Conversion was slow in starting. They looked at Peter, heavily built and strong, and inquired if he was not the leader of the party. Humphrey said no, and pointed to me. They were puzzled, looking first at Peter's bulky frame, then at my unathletic figure. They nodded among themselves. Finally one of them turned to me.

'You must be very intelligent,' he said.

We eventually learnt to sort out the three Mohammeds. There was Mohammed ben (son of) Ahmed, who said that if ever we wanted a mule, or even ten, we could have them free; he would arrange it. Then there was Mohammed ben Hamed, who only had one mule, but this too we could have whenever we wished. The third, Mohammed ben Ali, had no mules at all and made no promises. Later during our stay, when Humphrey wished to go to Taddert, he asked Mohammed ben Ahmed for a mule. But the story was then different. He 'could not possibly provide one for less than seven hundred francs'. In fact, three hundred and fifty francs was a fair price. Humphrey walked. Mohammed ben Hamed was nearer the truth; his free mule only cost us four hundred. We came to know these two as 'Mohammed-ten-mules' and 'Mohammed-one-mule'.

Another of our early visitors was Lhassan ben Idirh. The Sheikh had commanded him to provide us with bread. He came each day for the flour, which his wife baked in her open-air oven. Dung was much used as fuel, and, since the dough was placed directly upon the fire, our daily bread often had unpleasant accretions. For the first week or two we did our own cooking and washing-up, but we found that this was a very time-consuming activity and decided to employ someone from the village to do it for us. We noised it abroad that we were in need of this help, and Mohammed-ten-mules was one of the first applicants for the job. When he came down to discuss it we asked him about his health. He had, he said, been recently unwell and had journeyed down to the French doctor forty miles to the south. He proudly showed me the card which the doctor had given him. He clearly did not realize that it showed him to be suffering from tuberculosis. I felt it unwise to run the risk of employing him to prepare our food, and I must confess that it worried me a little when he came to visit the camp, since he was very fond of spitting. In order to avoid the embarrassment of turning him down directly, I said that I felt it would be diplomatic to employ our servants through the Sheikh.

We visited the Sheikh at his house in Anammer, and told him of our need for domestic help. A few days later we heard that a suitable candidate had been found. He was a youth of about seventeen whose name was Brahim, and who had visited Casablanca—a circumstance which gave him great prestige in the valley. The Sheikh's right-hand man came down to the camp clutching, as usual, his club, and said that he would bring Brahim down on the following day, '*Insha' Allah.*' He did not come at the promised time, but two days later he appeared with his candidate. We discussed terms of employment. The Sheikh's man did all the talking, and Brahim said not a word. The bargaining went on as follows.

'The boy is an excellent worker. He can speak French fluently. He will do exactly as you say.'

'I hope he understands that he will have to work very hard?'

'Of course. He is used to hard work. You will see that he is strong for his age.'

'We will offer him three hundred francs a day.'

'No, no. That is too much. He will be perfectly happy with two hundred.'

We finally agreed on a wage of two hundred and fifty, for the Sheikh was trying to impress us that he was looking after our interests—even to the extent of depriving Brahim of a fair wage. The agreement was made, and the boy still said nothing—probably the only period of sustained silence in his life. He was one of the noisiest young men I have ever met. We discovered that his 'fluent French' consisted of about six words, but he could make a very satisfactory imitation of a motor-car—a performance which he gave on every possible occasion.

Apart from our earliest acquaintances, the villagers kept very much to themselves. They were perfectly polite, but nevertheless suspicious. Then one day a man came down from Anammer in a very agitated state. His daughter had been badly scalded a few days before, and now had a high fever. Could we possibly help? I said that I would certainly examine her, and he brought her to the camp later in the evening. It was getting getting dark, and a thunderstorm was brewing. The high wind which preceded it was funnelled by the valley walls into a roaring gale. The lamp flickered, and dust was driven into the tent as I examined the girl. It was clearly impossible to get her to the French doctor in time, for her fever had risen to 105 degrees and she was becoming delirious. The scalds, which covered her back, were not only badly infected but coated with a thick black substance.

'What is it?' I asked.

'It is potato.'

I was puzzled, but he explained that scalds were always treated with a mixture of burnt potato and tea. It was a surprisingly sensible remedy, for it is only in recent years that tannin from tea has been superseded as a treatment recommended by doctors. The charcoal might serve a similar function to absorbent lint.

I told the girl's father that she was very likely to die, and that he must not hold me responsible if she did so. Nevertheless he begged me to treat her. Removing potato and charcoal from wounds by a flickering lamp in a howling dusty wind is a difficult task, but finally I managed to get the scalds into a reasonably aseptic condition, and I decided to give the girl an injection of penicillin. I had never given one before, and I was extremely nervous, since a hypodermic syringe can be a dangerous instrument in the hands of the uninitiated. I was terrified lest I should pierce a vein or artery. In order to reduce this hazard I injected her in the buttock, which contains few large blood-vessels.

I spent the next two days worrying about our patient, but on the third day her father came triumphantly into camp to tell us that she was completely cured. The following morning I saw her taking the cattle out to pasture.

This episode had the effect of breaking down the barriers of reserve between the villagers and ourselves, and it earned me my first invitation to dinner—to the house of the girl's father, Omar ben Hamed. We climbed up the steep path to his village. Small groups of men were sitting in the fields shouting, from time to time, to scare away the birds from their crops. The women crowded on the flat roofs as Omar shouted, 'The doctor is coming.' Villagers greeted us from every doorway. I squatted outside his mud and stone dwelling while preparations were made to receive me. He soon returned, and led me through a yard filled with excited children and chickens to a low oak door. Inside it was dark, and I could dimly see and strongly detect enormous piles of dung. We were on the ground floor where the cattle were housed at night and my host told me that they were kept here permanently during the winter. The houses were often snowed up for many weeks, he said, and the animals helped to keep them warm. I thought without relish of the state of the atmosphere at such times.

We clambered up a wooden ladder to the living-room above. Omar was a poor man, and his room was not whitewashed. The mud plaster flaked from the walls, the single window had no glass. A dirty mule-pack was heaped in one corner, and a threadbare carpet covered half the floor. There was no other furniture. He blew up a pottery brazier and put on the kettle for tea. We talked of life in the valley. He owned three of the terraced fields and grew maize, barley and millet. With his cows and chickens they produced enough to keep his family alive. He complained of the taxes levied by the Khalifa and of the depredations of the wild boar which came down at night to dig up the crops. But life was easier, he said, than in his father's time. In those days caravans passed through the Ait Rbaa on their way from Marrakesh to the Sahara. The men of his village made their living by trading salt, sugar and dates, and ranged from Fez in the north to the last oasis of the Draa. Those, too, were the days of furious tribal wars, of blood feuds and banditry, when no one was safe from sudden attack. All had been changed by the coming of the French. The road had been built, and the caravans no longer passed this way. Fighting had stopped. There was more time to farm and talk and drink tea with one's friends.

After tea he allowed his two wives to see the strange visitor. They stood at the far end of the room, looked curiously, but said nothing. The younger one was remarkably beautiful, with almond eyes, high cheek-bones and full lips. The other looked an old woman, although I learnt later that she was not yet thirty.

Berber women are in a much better position than their Arab sisters. They are not veiled, and they have much more say in the affairs of life. Among the mountain tribes a woman has laws to protect her, a right to the money she earns, and she can inherit under wills. There is an exception in that she cannot inherit land. Most characteristic, however, is a Berber woman's right to enter into a *sacred* bond or agreement, represented by the gift of the *anaya*. This is some symbolic object, perhaps a stick or stone, which passes between the parties to a contract. Far more Berbers than Arabs are monogamous. Among many tribes the eldest daughter's son succeeds to an inheritance. All these things suggest that the Berbers may originally have had, before the imposition of Islam, a matriarchal society.

Only one type of woman is really held in low esteem; the *kuata* or go-between, whose services are ostensibly employed in the task of arranging marriages, but who often, in fact, promotes less respectable liaisons. Even so, women are far from being considered the equals of men and do a great deal of the hard work, carrying heavy pots of water from the spring, working in the fields, taking the cattle out to pasture, as well as all the multitudinous duties of the home.

Our dinner started with pancakes fried in rancid oil, which we dipped in honey. I cannot say that they were pleasant to an uninitiated palate, and I was looking forward to the mutton stew. But this turned out to be a stew with a difference. My host had paid me a great compliment; he had honoured me by serving the 'sheep of the sacrifice', which had been slaughtered at the feast of Aid el Kebir. It was now some weeks after that celebration, and the taste was beyond description. To make matters worse the drying of the meat had given it a consistency exactly like rubber. It was very nearly impossible to bite, and one therefore could not swallow it quickly. It was necessary to chew for some considerable time, savouring the nauseating taste of decay.

The meal finished, my host rose to escort me home. Before leaving the house he pushed his wives into a room and locked the door with an enormous key which he kept hung round his neck. It was certain that they would be up to no mischief during his absence.

News of the startling recovery of Omar's daughter soon spread through the villages, and resulted in many demands for medicine. One of the commonest ailments seemed to be a general lassitude combined with pains in the joints. They called it *imuslmen,* and believed it to be caused by *djnun* (spirits, singular—*djinn*). The accepted treatment was to pierce the unfortunate patient with red-hot needles. This was supposed to make the *djinn* so uncomfortable that it hastily departed. We found that Epsom-salts had a similar effect.

The *djnun* of Berber belief seem to be somewhat different from those of orthodox Islam. They are reported to live everywhere, in stones and streams, in caves and even in people. They have the power to assume any form. They are evil, and yet they do not, so I was told in the village, come under the jurisdiction of *shaitan* (satan). The *djnun* rarely appear to human eyes, but there are many evidences of their activity. *Imuslmen* is only one of them. If a cow does not give milk or if it becomes wild, people will say that it is the work of a *djinn.* There are *djnun* of both sexes. The females of the species are of course the worst. The most famous of these is *Ayisha Kendisha*, who, to satisfy her appetite for human flesh, changes her form into that of a wife or fiancée, and lures men to their doom. One can tell the results of her work for she does not eat the head, hands, or feet. Then there is *Thaserount Isundahl*, 'the mule of the cemetery', who lives in grave-yards: during the day she has the form of a woman, but at nightfall changes into a mule. She rises from the grave 'shrieking horribly and dragging chains' and spends her evenings eating men. There is only one way to defeat her; by catching her round the neck and hanging on until daybreak, when she changes back into a woman.

Some men, notably the *talebs*—have power over the *djnun*. Nearly every village has a *taleb* who has been educated at a religious school and who can read and write. He has religious duties, reading from the Koran and officiating in the mosque. His services are paid by subscrip-tions from the villagers and he is often rich. The *talebs* of southern Morocco are famous for their ability at magic, and those of the Sous region are supposed to be particularly good. C. M. Doughty, in his *Arabia Deserta*, speaks of them:

'The Moors . . . are esteemed in Arabia the best scriveners of magical scriptures and the people suppose them to be of a wonderful subtlety in the finding of hidden treasures.' Sous magicians were famous even before Islam came to Morocco. The finding of lost treasure seems always to have been their speciality. M'Barek told us that he had seen one of these magicians at work. A thief had stolen several sacks of corn from his village granaries. The *taleb* was called in. He employed a small boy to act as a medium. A fire was made in a pottery brazier, incense was thrown upon it, and the boy stood with his palms out-stretched over it. Burnt wool and written prayers from the Koran were placed in his hands. The *taleb* murmured incantations. Suddenly the boy shouted out that he could see the granary and a man creeping into it. He described the culprit and then told where the stolen grain was hidden. The villagers went to the place he described and found the missing corn. The thief confessed and was punished.

Belief in magic is widespread in Morocco, the villains usually being either women or *djnun*. Many women are believed to possess the evil eye, and there is a well-known proverb: 'What the devil does in a year, an old woman does in an hour.'

There are, as well as the *talebs* and family magicians, many other sorcerers of various degrees of wickedness. The Pasha of Marrakesh was reputed to have a magician who protected him from bullets. There are those in Morocco, as well as elsewhere, who read palms, or the arrangement of hair on the head. The Jews have a considerable reputation in the preparation of love potions.

There are, too, a number of fabulous beasts; particularly famous is the mountain lion of the Middle Atlas which rubs itself against its victim in the manner of a cat, and so entices him to its den—and his doom.

While the unpleasant effects of *djnun* were widespread, I was often faced with more serious cases, such as that of Ayisha. I first came across her sitting, with her husband Mohammed ben Embark, outside a small stone hut on the mountain side opposite Idirh. In this place had lived a holy man, and the hut was supposed to possess very powerful *baraka*. Each morning her husband brought Ayisha from the village of Titullah on the back of his mule, for she was too weak to walk. He begged me to treat her. She was a pale, beautiful girl about sixteen years of age, and she rested weakly against the wall while I questioned her. This proved to be a laborious process, since it is not considered seemly for an unmarried man to talk to another man's wife. I therefore had to address my inquiries in French to M'Barek, who passed them in Arabic to Mohammed, who then questioned his wife in Berber, since the women do not speak Arabic.

I suspected distortions when the conversation progressed as follows:

'Have you had any pain?'

'Twice.'

'Do you mean twice today?'

'No, I have two children.'

'Do—you—have—any—pain—*now*?'

'Yes. It is coming in four months.'

At length I got the facts. Ayisha was indeed very sick. I took her husband aside.

'She must go at once to the French doctor,' I said.

'I cannot afford to make the journey.'

'I will give you money.'

'The crops must be harvested, I cannot go.'

'She is in danger of death.'

'If God wills it, she will die. Who am I to question the will of God?'

My entreaties were in vain. I could not persuade him to go. His attitude was not born of enmity towards his wife. Such a reluctance to visit the town for treatment was widespread. It was partly for fear of destroying the beneficial effects of the saints' *baraka*, partly for fear of being sent to hospital and separated from friends and families. The French doctor, when later I saw him, explained this to me. Many villagers, he said, lose the will to live when they are sent to hospital in Marrakesh. They preferred to treat their diseases themselves, or to consult the *talebs*.

Talebs, as well as being able to control the *djnun*, also use drugs and herbs for the treatment of disease. Some of the remedies are frightening. M'Barek told me of a woman who was instructed to drink kerosene to procure a child. Stork-meat and eggs are also considered efficacious. Snakes' hearts, eaten, ensure that the child will be a boy. Burnt animal horns are good for boils and scabs. Various kinds of snail are prescribed for coughs, typhoid fever, and corns! Wounds were cauterized with burnt cloth. There were a number of dried plants, which unfortunately we were unable to identify, used in the treatment of constipation and dysentery. The Moroccan pharmacopoeia is endless. Some of the treatments, like that for burns, were surprisingly sensible. Others could be explained in terms of sympathetic magic, but the majority seemed to be completely fortuitous. The villagers' knowledge of anatomy was poor. Mohammed-one-mule, for instance, imagined that the tendons of the hand were vessels carrying water.

As time went by we came to know more and more of the inhabitants of Idirh, and we began to be accepted as members of the community. Humphrey spent a great deal of time in the village. His programme of research involved the study of its social structure, and its inhabitants were indulgent in answering questions which were often of a very personal nature. A similar investigation in an English village would have caused a minor riot. Humphrey learnt a great deal about the day-to-day life of the tribesmen.

The people of the Ait Rbaa belong to the Glaoua tribe from which springs the ruling Glaoui family. At the time of our visit the tribe was governed, at any rate in theory, by Caid Brahim, the eldest son of the Pasha, who ruled from Telouet an area equal to that of Yorkshire. This area was divided into a number of smaller units each administered by a Khalifa. The Khalifa at Telouet was responsible for the north Glaoua—the region which included our valley. The khalifates were further divided into a number of *fractions* of four or five villages. Each *fraction* was commanded by a Sheikh, and each village had a headman, or Mokkadem. In some ways these officials had absolute power. An example of this has already been mentioned: the Khalifa of Telouet providing us with our caravan of mules.

The taxes levied by the Pasha's administration were heavy. A posse of sheikhs and soldiers toured the region several times a year to collect them, and it was accepted that minor officials were entitled to a share. Crimes were punished ruthlessly. The people in the village were in fear lest any of our equipment be stolen, for then, they said, twenty suspects would be taken and beaten unconscious. We lost nothing.

In spite of this seemingly tyrannical rule the tribesmen were largely content, and they called themselves *Imaziren*, the Free People. In some way, they took pleasure in subordination, in denying the body in order to emphasize their equality in spirit. Consequently the relation between chieftain and tribesman was at the same time more free and more subject than elsewhere. Servants were afraid of punishment not only because it was painful, but because it was a symbol to which their obedience was vowed. They had a freedom of consent to yield to their master the most abject service because in spirit they were equal to him, and to this extent at any rate the service was voluntary. If the administration displeased them they could resist, and they did not live in fear of death and pain. Death and pain were too common to be overvalued. I saw villagers stand unflinching with injuries that would have reduced most Europeans to unconsciousness.

This spiritual freedom existing between master and servant was not the only reason that the tribesmen felt themselves to be free. The power of the Pasha's administration, although great, by no means covered every aspect of their existence. Within the villages they could to a large extent organize their own lives in the way which suited them best. There were, as we shall see later, even elements of democracy in village life.

Idirh had about twenty houses. Looking at the village it would be impossible to know this, since most of them were joined erratically together. I use the word 'house' for want of a better one, but these bore in fact a closer resemblance to maisonettes. The first floor of one family's dwelling was quite often above the ground floor belonging to another. The three 'rich' families in the village had separate establishments with walled courtyards. Mohammed-one-mule, although he was poor, also had a house set apart from the others. The population of the village was about two hundred; in other words, there was an average of ten people to each house of about four rooms.

There was one small shop in the village, where sugar, tea, coffee, dates, and carbide could be bought; assuming, that is, that the shopkeeper took the trouble to borrow mules and go to the stores at Taddert. It was only a minute hovel of a room, with a counter made of tea-chests, but it faced the small open space at the centre of the village, and five or six men sitting on top of each other could just squeeze in to pass the time of day. Here, squatting on sacks while buyers kicked aside children to lean in from the doorway and make their purchases, one could hear who was getting married, what the latest prices were, the news of incidents in the towns, and any scandal picked up at the market. The shop was one of Humphrey's earliest contacts with the village, and it was in the shop that he learnt when anyone was ploughing or when threshing was in progress.

The terraced fields belonging to the village had been scratched and scooped out of the soil on the lower slopes along the stream. Maize, barley, rye, millet, roots and Indian hemp were grown on its narrow strips. Ploughing was an intricate job. Carrying the back-breaking water-jars, herding and milking the cows, fetching firewood down the mountain side, and gathering reeds for fodder were all jobs done by women; but ploughing was man's work.

The frame of the plough itself was of wood, but the ploughshare was a spade-shaped piece of hammered iron. The whole affair could be dismantled into three sections so that it was easily carried up the steep paths from one terraced field to the next. When it was assembled its single shaft was attached between two mules, and the pair would work back and forth on a piece of land the size of a postage stamp. It was a difficult job, but the terraces were ploughed and not a scrap of fertile earth was wasted in this infertile valley.

The fields were watered by a complicated network of *seguias*, or irrigation ditches, fed from mountain springs. Every available drop of water was utilized and it was long a puzzle to us how its distribution was regulated. We knew that it *was* regulated: a system had been worked out in three days, when the road was built, the mule trade finished, and the Ait Rbaa turned to farming in earnest. It was a ponderously complicated system, and however carefully each man was allotted his immutable quantity of water, co-operative effort was involved. New ditches had to be dug, old ones repaired, and in times of drought or flood special conditions obviously required some kind of general assembly to discuss what should be done, since irrigation was not within the jurisdiction of the Sheikh. This was the crux of the problem, for everyone claimed that there was no such thing as an assembly. Yet each man knew at what time he was entitled to divert water to his fields. 'Everyone knows what should happen,' they said. The problem was resolved when we learnt in passing that such topics were often discussed at the weekly meeting in the mosque. This was the assembly for which we were searching. It was a form of organization so habitual that no one was conscious of its existence.

The fields provided enough to feed the inhabitants of the village and there was some land to spare for the growth of cash crops. The most important of these was Indian hemp. Under French law it was illegal to grow the plant, whose only commercial value lies in its leaves, from which the drug hashish is made, but French officials very rarely came to the Ait Rbaa. Hashish fetched a high price in the markets of Marrakesh. One could get Fr. 1,000 (£1) per kilogram, and an average field produced eighty kilograms per year. The Pasha's administration was well aware of the hemp-growing, and each year an official came to the valley to collect taxes. These taxes usually amounted to thirty per cent of the profit on the crop, but nevertheless it was still a money-making proposition. The Pasha clearly derived a considerable part of his income from the sale of narcotics. Nevertheless it would be unwise to judge him too harshly, since it could well be argued that the effects of hashish-smoking are no worse than those of drink. Large numbers of southern Moroccans smoke the drug (which is locally known as *kief*), but few are confirmed addicts.

Soon after our arrival the tax-collectors came to the village and in that year the taxes were higher than usual. There was a great deal of hard feeling in the valley, and rumour had it that the official was taking too heavy a percentage for his own use. In one of the villages further down the valley, in fact, he was stoned by angry inhabitants.

Other crops were also taxed, but not at the same high rate. In addition, the Pasha derived income from levies of various kinds. To have permission to own a gun, for instance, a tribesman was obliged to pay the Khalifa about thirty-thousand francs. If he wished to leave the valley to work in the north at harvest-time he must get permission from the Khalifa, and must pay for the privilege by first cutting the

Pasha's corn or by working for a certain time at the *kasbah*. Whenever one of the officials from Telouet visited a village, he must be liberally entertained at the expense of the inhabitants.

As well as cultivating the fields the people of Idirh kept various kinds of livestock. There were a few cows and chickens, but far greater numbers of sheep and goats. It was the custom that the younger sons of each family lived out on the mountains grazing the flocks, which wandered over great distances in their search for suitable food. It is probable that the sparsity of vegetation in the Atlas can be attributed, to a large extent, to the activity of sheep and goats.

In the late autumn there was a great migration from the mountains down into the Sahara. During the winter the desert received a little rain, and for two or three months it was suitable for grazing. The tribes took advantage of this, and the younger sons drove the sheep a distance of 200 miles to the feeding-grounds.

*   *   *   *

The speed with which we got to know people in Idirh was inversely related to their wealth and social status. It was not, I suppose, unreasonable. Initially we tried to follow the customs of the country and to give food to all our visitors. The poorer people had most to gain from this, and they came in ever-increasing numbers. It was made clear to us, however, that there were three 'respected men' whom we should visit, three men who dominated the affairs of the village, and whose answers were most likely to resolve our problems concerning the agriculture and history of the community. The Ait Rbaa is a poor area, and there are no palatial castles or elaborate houses to cater for a life of ease. Outwardly there was little to distinguish these three men, but they were rich to the point of security, which was unusual. Two of them had been able to make the pilgrimage to Mecca, and therefore were addressed by the title 'Hadj'. The third was the *taleb*.

We met Si Hadj Lhassan one clear morning, coming up from his fields with an adze over his shoulder. He had a sharp, lean face which betrayed his keen intelligence. Apologizing for the scanty reception he could give us, he invited us into his home. It was very like the other houses in the village, but demonstrated the opulence of its owner in having a large square window which was protected by a complicated wrought-iron grid, and which even contained a plate of glass. The expenditure of money on putting in windows was, in the Ait Rbaa, what the sociologists would call 'conspicuous consumption'. Rich Americans have Cadillacs; rich Berbers have windows.

Hadj Lhassan received us in a small mud-plastered and completely bare room above the door. He bundled in a black and white village rug, which he spread on the floor, and called for a boy to blow up the brazier for tea. We talked of the path that led up the valley, over the high col and south to Telouet, and the Hadj told us about the time when this path had been part of the great caravan route from Marrakesh to the Sahara. The caravaneers had come through the valley with mules, camels and slaves, and at night they had found lodgings in the villages. He well remembered this route in the times before the French had built the road and finished the trade for ever. Like everyone else he had made quick money running his mules with salt and sugar to the south, and back with dates to the north.

He became nostalgic about the days of *siba*—the days when the mountains and the semi-desert beyond remained in the hands of tribal chieftains, or of small independent communities which were ruled by ancient custom and which fought among themselves; the days when every traveller carried a gun. Then he pulled himself together and said, like Omar, that things were better now.

We did not meet the second rich man until his wife fell ill. He asked me to treat her. His name was Boghrib and it was rumoured that he was the richest man in the village. He was reported to own more than one thousand sheep and goats. Certainly his house had more windows than Hadj Lhassan's, and the carpets on which we sat were richer and more exotic. After the inevitable mint-tea he called in his wife so that I could examine her. She was a beautiful woman, and I was embarrassed to discover that she had an infection of the breast. I treated her as best I could, covering the sore places with lint and bands of elastoplast. This breast infection turned out to be common among the women of the village, and when Boghrib's wife improved in health I had a number of other demands for treatment. This gave rise to a good deal of ribald comment among my companions about, 'Bryan's brassières for Berbers'.

Conversation with Boghrib turned to the subject of the French. I discovered that he disliked them vehemently. His brother, he said, had served in the French Army and had been killed during the fighting in Tunisia. Boghrib believed that as a result of this he himself was entitled to a pension, but the French had not given him one. M'Barek, who was also present, and whose father had been a sergeant in the French Army, had a similar tale to tell. After his father had retired he had taken his pension-book one day to the bureau to collect his money, and a French official had taken the book 'so that it could be stamped'. It was never given back. Boghrib was probably not entitled to a pension, but M'Barek's seems to have been a case of genuine injustice.

In England before we left, the newspapers had suggested that Nationalism in Morocco was not a truly popular movement. But the longer we stayed, the more convinced I became that it was a strong and genuine force. Terrorism, bomb-throwing, and similar activities may have been acts of fanatics, but even this was not always so, as we discovered later. Even in the Ait Rbaa, in the Pasha's own tribe, opinion about the French was divided. Some said: 'To be a Glaoua is to be a Frenchman,' or: 'We are ready for war. We will fight with the French against the rest of Morocco.' But these were public statements. In private I heard whispered complaints against the French; some of the villagers were unhappy because they could not get education for their children. There were even faint murmurings against the Pasha, but these were most secret of all. Boghrib, it seemed, was not alone in his dislikes.

We met the *taleb*, the third of the respected men, last of all, and on first acquaintance he seemed hostile. This was not altogether unexpected. The *talebs*, being usually the only people who can read and write Arabic, are often the most politically conscious. Furthermore, because of their religious duties they tend to be fanatical Muslims. Both these factors combine to make them suspicious of Europeans. Also, perhaps, he did not approve of our poaching on his medical preserves. The time came, however, when he developed a bad stomach-ache. So he swallowed his pride, followed by several of our pills, and friendly relations were established. Our acquaintance with the *taleb* was also improved when M'Barek agreed to give him lessons in mathematics. M'Barek, although he was only eighteen, had enormous prestige among the villagers; not only could he read and write, he could speak the language of the Christians. People addressed him respectfully as 'Sidi', a title reserved for persons of exalted position.

Without M'Barek's help we certainly could not have achieved even what little we did during our stay at Idirh. He worked incredibly hard, and remained cheerful even under the most trying circumstances. He was perpetually in demand as an interpreter: Humphrey needed him, of course, for his work in the village; Peter required his services to find details of the ownership of fields; John and I were always asking him to help us in our collections. We taught him to treat the patients so that we could devote more time to our own work. In addition he was our constant adviser on behaviour and etiquette. When we first met him we had made it clear that we were not well-informed about good manners in Moroccan society, and that he must correct us whenever we committed a *faux pas*. Often, at some social function or other, we would say to him:

'Please say whatever you think is polite.'

He must have done his job well, for I discovered that we had developed a reputation in the village for observing the niceties of Berber customs. A man said to me:

'You are not like the French. You are not rude to us; you do not shout at us.'

Another said: 'You are very delicate.'

This might have been a backhander, but I *think* it was designed as a compliment.

M'Barek, too, told us a great deal about his religion, and we had long discussions on the relative merits of Islam and Christianity. He took a more tolerant view of the Christians than did most Muslims. This may have been due to his education under Christian teachers.

'After all,' he said, 'we worship the same God. We have the same traditions about events before the birth of the Prophet. We differ only about the relative status of Christ and the Prophet. Muslims do not deny that Jesus Christ was a holy man, we only deny His divinity—and does not the Koran say: "You will find the most affectionate friends will be those who say, 'We are Christians'?"

'We agree that God is the Creator of the universe, that Jesus was miraculously born, and that He ascended into heaven. We agree that there is a Holy Spirit and that God will forgive men's sins and grant them everlasting life. I cannot subscribe to your religion, but it is nearer to ours than many would think.'

I was myself surprised at the similarities, but of course I imagine that many Muslims would be equally surprised. It must be remembered, however, that late in his life the Prophet may have modified his attitude towards Christians. In another part of the Koran he says: 'May God fight them; how perverse they are,' but it is possible that this refers only to those Christians who are not faithful to their scriptures.

G

The religious observances practised in Morocco are similar to those
of the rest of Islam, at any rate among the Arabs. The most important
ritual duties are prayer, almsgiving, fasting, and the pilgrimage. There
are five traditional times for prayer: at sunset, during the night, at
dawn, noon, and in the afternoon. People are called to their devotions
by the *muezzin*, who mounts a minaret of the mosque and shouts out
his penetrating cry: 'God is most great. I testify that there is no God
but Allah, and that Mohammed is His Prophet. Come to prayer,
come to security. God is most great.'

In each mosque there is a recess in the direction of which the worshipper must face, because then he is facing Mecca. At the beginning of
prayers the Muslim opens his hands and, touching the lobes of his ears
with the thumbs, he says, 'God is great.' Lowering his hands and
folding them, he then recites the first chapter of the Koran.

'In the name of Allah, the Compassionate, the Merciful. Praise be to
Allah, Lord of the creation, the Compassionate, the Merciful, King of
the last judgement. You alone we worship, and to you alone we pray
for help. Guide us to the straight path, the path of those whom you
have favoured, not of those who have incurred your wrath, nor of
those who have gone astray.'

Other verses may follow. Then the worshipper bows and says: 'The
perfection of the Lord, the Great,' and he rises again, chanting
'God is great', sinks gently to his knees, and prostrates himself with his
face to the ground. In this position he uses the same words as before.
This ritual may be repeated any number of times. At the end of his
prayers he looks over his right shoulder and says:

'Peace be unto you, and the mercy of Allah.' Then he says the same
words over his left shoulder.

In large gatherings of people complete uniformity is obtained during
the prostrations by appointing an *Imam* who leads the prayers.

Fasting is another important practice of Muslims, and the Koran lays
down that it should continue throughout the month of *Ramadan*.
During *Ramadan* no one may eat, drink, or smoke between sunrise and
sunset. This can be a very serious discomfort when the month of fasting
falls in the summer, and when—as in Marrakesh during the hot wind
—the temperature may rise above 115 degrees F. Sick people are
exempted from this observance, but they are required to fast for an
equal number of days when their health has improved.

All Muslims are expected at some time in their lives to make the

Hadj, or Pilgrimage to Mecca, and to visit the Prophet's tomb. Drinking alcohol and eating pig are rigorously forbidden. These are the strict observances of Islam, and the Arabs of Morocco are assiduous in maintaining them.

The Berbers, however, have a reputation for being less zealous. It has been said: 'The Berber is not a Muslim; he only thinks he is.' Berbers are reputed not to observe the prescribed ritual ablutions of Islam, to break the fast at *Ramadan*, to eat the meat of wild boar, and to drink fig-brandy. They are reputed to do so, but in our valley we heard only of failures on the last two counts.

I have already mentioned that the cult of saints is stronger among the Berbers than elsewhere, and that doubtless it springs from more ancient beliefs.

Each group in the Berber social organization has its own particular saint. The saints of *fractions* or villages may be obscure men known only in a very restricted area. Nevertheless, their *baraka* is reputedly powerful in guarding the flocks or improving the crops, and young girls will come to their tombs in order to learn to weave or spin without effort. Married women mounted on a mule will ride seven times round a tomb in order to get rid of evil influences. This ritual was probably performed by Mohammed ben Embark's wife at the hut opposite Idirh. The *marabouts* of tribes are more celebrated, and their *baraka* is correspondingly more powerful. Near their tombs there are often settlements of their descendants, who are supposed to inherit some of the saint's goodwill. These settlements may be in the form of religious fraternities, or *zaouias*. Then there are saints of wider renown, to whose sanctuaries pilgrims travel many hundreds of miles to implore their protection, to vow vengeance on enemies, or to seek refuge from pursuit.

At certain times of the year great gatherings of people come together at the resting places of important saints for religious festivals, or *moussems*; and singing, dancing and feasting may last for several days. It is rarely that Europeans have attended a *moussem*, and we tried to persuade the villagers to take us to an important one which was due to occur somewhere south of the Atlas. But they clearly did not wish us to go, and told us conflicting stories of its date and locality. After it happened we met several people who had been to the festival, but they would tell us no details.

CHAPTER SEVEN

Pillars of the Sky

Once more at a distance of ten day's journey there is a salt hill, a spring, and a tract of inhabited country, and adjoining it rises Mount Atlas. In shape the mountain is a slender cone, and it is so high that according to report the top cannot be seen, because summer and winter it is never free of cloud. The natives (who are known as the Atlantes, after the mountain) call it the 'Pillar of the Sky'. They are said to eat no living creature, and never to dream.

HERODOTUS

THE time came when the people of the villages began to know us individually and to call us by name. I was known throughout the valley as 'M'Soor Chef'—an unfortunate appellation which conjured up visions of a white-capped Gaul in a steaming kitchen.

They had difficulty in pronouncing the names of the others. Humphrey was their greatest problem. They tried for some time to pronounce his Christian name, but eventually despaired of it and resorted to referring to him as 'M'Soor Bayket'. John became 'M'Soor Yown', and Peter 'M'Soor Bayta'.

As we were given names we also developed reputations. Humphrey was noted for his curiosity, for he was perpetually asking the most searching and personal questions. I was known more for my medical activities, and also for being a leader who seemed to have remarkably little say in the conduct of our affairs. John became famous for his sense of direction, or the lack of it. This was unjust, stemming from the single occasion on which he got lost. He went out one day to make the first ascent of the nearby mountain Djebel Tistouit, and did not get back to the valley until after dark. He lost himself a few hundred yards to the south of Idirh, and was not rescued until Mohammed ben Ali heard his shouts and led him home. Peter was well-known, justly in this case, for his strength and silence.

Our camp, as I have mentioned, was situated in the shade of a large walnut tree about two hundred feet below the village. There were two tents: a large one, about twelve feet long, with a central ridgepole; and a small bell-tent. The former was used as an office and laboratory where we could write up our notes in the evenings, and where John and I could prepare our specimens away from the wind and the dust. The smaller tent was used to house stores. We slept out under the stars. It very rarely rained at night, and we enjoyed sleeping in the open. One could lie in bed and listen to the faint voices of late travellers, singing as they climbed the winding paths, to the gurgle of water in the irrigation ditches, and to the occasional cry of a fox or jackal. We felt at home under our walnut tree.

Later when the camp had become a public meeting-place, and we were liable to have visitors at almost any time of the day or night, we began to feel the need for privacy. People would appear at the most embarrassing moments, and I did not enjoy getting dressed in front of an interested crowd of spectators. I had an automatic razor, which worked by pumping with the hand, and this always drew a large audience, who would gaze with rapture while I removed my morning beard. In order to remedy the situation we erected a tarpaulin screen, but it was not a success, since people could very easily walk around it. They invariably did. We also found it necessary to erect some kind of shelter where I could treat patients, particularly the women patients, away from the public eye. We used the flysheet of the little tent.

Cooking was largely done by Peter. Although we arranged a roster for domestic duties, the concoctions produced by the rest of us were so unpleasant that Peter was obliged to do most of the work. I made myself very unpopular by steadfastly refusing to rise early and prepare breakfast. It was selfish, but I have always found it hard to get up in the morning.

Before the arrival of Brahim our domestic activities took up a great deal of time, and it was a relief to have somebody who would do the washing-up. Brahim, however, was a mixed blessing. His six words of French and his imitations of motor-cars became very tiring after we had heard them the first hundred times. He had boundless energy and great enthusiasms, not the least of which concerned his love-life. Many of the villagers tended to be indiscriminate in their amorous activities, and we had trouble with a number of them who developed attachments to Brahim. Lhassan ben Idirh was one of the major culprits. He came often to the camp in the evening to inquire if Brahim could not accompany him to assist in guarding the hashish fields. It was very necessary at this time of the year, he said, since there were men who would steal the crop during the night.

Brahim must have led a full life, for we often heard in embarrassing detail of his more normal, if not more respectable activities with the ladies of the village. Indeed, the *kuata*, or go-between—a vast lady of indeterminate age—gave him a message for us:

'If,' she said, 'you particularly desire any of the women in the village I shall be happy to arrange a liaison. The fee will be two hundred and fifty francs.'

The offer, we were told, included any of the married women, but perhaps the *kuata* was merely boasting. I do not know what would have been the feelings of husbands about such arrangements. We did not consider it discreet to inquire.

Life in the camp was peaceful. Now that we had settled down there were no longer the quarrels which had troubled us on the journey. Each of us went about his business and we often met only in the evenings. Time meant nothing, and we soon lost track of the days and weeks. It is difficult, in looking back, to arrange things in their proper chronological order. We would get up in the morning soon after sunrise, and eat a leisurely breakfast. Peter would then set off with planetable, compasses and clinometers to draw his map. Humphrey would make his way to the village. John would depart into the surrounding hills to collect his plants. I would remain in camp to deal with the dozen or more patients that appeared every morning.

They came with every conceivable kind of disease; tuberculosis, dysentery, fevers, boils, syphilis, rheumatism, and various forms of injury. There were many with trachoma—the terrible disease of the eyes which is so common in Morocco, and which is spread on the feet of flies. The majority of Moors allow these insects to walk unhindered across their eyeballs. I tried to discourage the villagers from doing this, but I did not have a great deal of success. There was nothing that I could do at that time about the trachoma, since the only effective treatment is the antibiotic aureomycin, which is expensive and difficult to obtain. For the majority of my patients I could do nothing but tell them to go to the French doctor. I do not believe that any of them did. In a few cases my treatments were genuinely effective.

It was the habit of the villagers when they wanted medicine to come beforehand with a gift. It would be perhaps a chicken, or half a dozen eggs, or some fruit. The size of the gift would depend both upon the severity of the illness and the wealth of the patient. Since I could very often do little to help them, I tried to persuade them not to bring these things, but they persisted. I felt guilty in accepting a chicken when all I could give in return was a couple of aspirins, but sometimes even aspirin did seem to have most remarkable curative powers.

Usually, it was midday before I had finished my 'surgery' and I would have a quick lunch of oatmeal biscuits and coffee, and then set out to search for animals. Most often I was alone, but sometimes M'Barek or Brahim would accompany me. I was most interested in the smaller animals and spent a lot of time collecting insects among the oaks on the upper slopes of the mountains. Other productive places were the dry stream-beds which branched out from the Ait Rbaa, and the many mountain springs. I collected large numbers of earthworms, which seemed to thrive in places where the mules were brought to water. Colin and I developed a theory that the earthworm eggs were carried from place to place on the feet of these animals! There were brightly-coloured butterflies and moths which flew erratically over the rocks, as well as innumerable grasshoppers. Enormous dragonflies were common near the streams. On the dry hillsides, under stones, one could find small red scorpions, large poisonous centipedes, and black hunting spiders. Lizards and snakes were common in the stream-beds, where there were boulders big enough to afford them protection. Other lizards lived in the high oakwoods—great green beasts, some of them four feet long.

There was one area near the pass to Telouet where ground-squirrels were common. These belonged to a species found only in the Atlas mountains. They were about a foot long, with two dark stripes on their backs, and they looked rather like American chipmunks, except that their tails were larger and bushier. I tried to catch one, but without success, for they were very quick little animals and apparently capable of vanishing into solid rock. Nor were they to be fooled by the traps I laid for them.

I tried to encourage the villagers to collect animals, and drew up a list of prices I would pay for various specimens, ranging from poison-ous snakes (7s. 6d.) to grasshoppers (six for 1d.). There was no great response; one or two people brought in specimens, but they would not accept money.

'We do not sell *animals*,' they said haughtily.

The children were more co-operative. They would bring specimens, usually mutilated, in exchange for boiled sweets. They heard that I collected scorpions and brought them to me alive. The children had little cloth purses about two inches square, with drawstrings, and they filled them with scorpions until they bulged. A child would turn one upside-down into my collecting jar, and ten or twelve scorpions would fall out. I did not discover how they managed to get so many in without being stung. In fact, although these animals are extremely common I did not meet anybody who had been bitten by one. Peter came nearest to it. One day, he was sitting in camp reading, when suddenly he jumped up and said: 'There's something crawling up my trouser leg.' He stamped his foot, and a large scorpion fell out. The animal paid for its temerity; it was immediately slain and preserved in alcohol.

From time to time I would take one of the shotguns to hunt larger animals. We had supplies of cartridges with different weights of shot, and I had ordered some filled with dust so that I could shoot lizards and snakes without damaging them too severely. I had, however, neglected to ask the manufacturers to reduce the charge of explosive, and the first time I went hunting, seeing a lizard sitting on a rock about five yards away, I took careful aim and fired. The lizard disintegrated completely, and I could not find even the smallest piece of it. All that remained was a rather nasty stain on the rock. After this, when I saw a lizard I would have to turn about, run back ten yards, and then shoot at it, aiming off slightly so that only a small amount of shot would hit it. Hunting in this manner was unproductive, since by the time I had retreated to a sufficient distance the lizard had usually disappeared.

My assaults upon birds were similarly unsuccessful. There were, on the western slopes of the valley, large coveys of partridges which came down at sunset to feed in the fields. The villagers asked us to shoot them, and we were very willing to comply, not only in the interests of local economy but also for the pot. They were difficult to shoot; very rarely rising on the wing, and tending merely to run behind the nearest rock. Since they were protectively coloured it was then almost impossible to find them. Sportsmanship at first prevented me from shooting unless they flew, but later I became completely unscrupulous, and would fire at a partridge if it so much as peeped over a rock. Even so, it was far more economical in partridges than in shot.

As at Djebel bou Ourioul, there were many hawks, and we tried to slay the largest of them, the great Lammergeyers which soared over the mountain tops. But they always seemed to remain just out of range.

On one exciting occasion I came across a big eagle sitting in a tree. The range was about fifteen yards, and I used a cartridge of the heaviest shot, normally reserved for deer and other large mammals, I took careful aim, and fired. A single feather fell from the eagle's tail. The bird turned its head, gave me a withering glance, and flew ponderously away.

The only animals which really excited the interest of the tribesmen were the *mouflon* (wild sheep), and the wild boar. The *mouflon* were timid creatures, living in the highest and most inaccessible parts of the range, and only coming down into the valleys during the coldest part of the winter. Mohammed-one-mule showed me the skin of a wild sheep which he had caught at Idirh—trapped in a snowdrift. The *mouflon* were reported to be very good eating, but we saw them only rarely, perched on some rocky outcrop or scrambling across the scree on the opposite side of a valley.

The villagers were interested in the wild boar not because they were good eating, but because they came down at night to dig for food and to destroy the crops. There was a particularly large and ferocious boar which lived on the mountain opposite Idirh, and which caused much damage. They begged us to shoot it, and John and I decided to spend a night on the mountain in the hope of tracking it down.

It was a foolish excursion. We only had shotguns, and even with the heaviest cartridge we would not be able to kill the boar at a range of more than seven yards. This meant waiting until it charged, and then we would have only one shot each.

On the day of our expedition John set out early to reconnoitre the area, and I followed in the afternoon with Brahim. Although I had loaded him with a knapsack, a butterfly net, a gun, and two water bottles, Brahim soon left me behind on the steep climb. He would wait patiently until I had caught up, then rush off again at enormous speed, grinning with delight.

We passed several young shepherds grazing their flocks on the scrubby slopes. They greeted us politely, but we had difficulty in avoiding the attentions of their ferocious dogs. The Atlas dogs are no household pets; they are ravening beasts. When entering a village it was wise to collect a handful of stones to keep them at bay.

We reached our rendezvous with John in good time, and Brahim returned home. We could hear him singing lustily long after he had disappeared from sight. We put down our bedding in a sheltered hollow and cooked supper on the Primus. From our bivouac we could see the whole valley spread out below us, and as the sun set it glowed with the intense colours of evening. We could see little figures returning to the village from their day's work. Snatches of song drifted up on the evening air. With darkness, small lights appeared all over the valley. In one of the villages there must have been a celebration, for the throbbing of drums continued until well after midnight.

The sky clouded over and the night became completely black. We could see nothing of the surrounding rocks, and the boar, if he were there, had us at a disadvantage. We listened.

John was asleep and I had just begun to doze when a rattle of stones brought me sharply to my senses. Another rattle, then a grunt. It was the boar, and he was coming towards us. I prodded John vigorously to wake him up. I must have prodded too hard, for he imagined that some animal—perhaps the boar—had jumped on him in the darkness. He rose up with an ear-splitting shout, which frightened both me and the boar, then there was silence. We waited. A while later we heard the beast again, snuffling and grunting around our little camp. We crept out of the hollow towards the sound. Then I dislodged a rock, which thundered down the scree, taking others on its way. We heard the boar retreating in the distance. Finally we returned to the hollow and fell asleep.

We woke to the sun streaming over the hills, casting huge shadows on the far side of the glen. Women were singing as they cut firewood on the lower slopes. When we came down into the valley other women were busy carrying water-jars to and from the spring, and little girls were shouting at slow-moving groups of cattle on their way to the pastures. There was not a man to be seen.

The news of our lack of success with the boar was received with sympathy, but I understand that there were comments in the village about 'men with expensive guns who could not shoot', and we afterwards had many requests for the loan of firearms.

Apart from exceptional occasions like the boar-hunt, we usually congregated in camp at nightfall and cooked the largest meal of the day. Often there were visitors who shared our food. The most frequent ones were Lhassan and the three Mohammeds.

After the meal had been cleared away we would spend the rest of the evening in the big tent writing up notes and cataloguing specimens by the light of the paraffin pressure lamp. The lamp attracted hundreds of insects, which provided some very welcome additions to my collections. Moths, of course, were the most common, and there were a number of impressive varieties, including hawk-moths with a wing-span of three inches. They would fly in through the entrance of the tent, strike the lamp, and fall to the earth. One of the local toads developed the habit of coming in each evening to gobble up the dazed insects.

Often we would be invited for a meal to a house in Idirh. One day Mohammed-one-mule came down to visit us.

'We will have a lottery,' he said. 'Write your name upon a piece of paper and I will write mine on another. Then we shall bury the papers. M'Barek will dig them up, and the person whose name is found first must give tea to the others.'

His name was drawn, and he was obliged to invite us to his house.

It was, as I have mentioned, set apart from the others, but it showed no evidence of riches. The windows were mere slits in the walls and the rooms dark and smoky. There were no carpets, but we sat on woven rush mats.

He told us a sad story about Mohammed-ten-mules, and his hashish crop.

'Last week,' he said, 'Mohammed ben Ahmed's *kief* was ready for sale. He decided to take it to Marrakesh. It was difficult, of course, because the French do not like us to sell the *kief*. But he wrapped it in cloth, so that it looked like a bundle of clothes, and he set off on the bus from Taddert. The man who sat next to him on the journey had a sensitive nose, and half-way to Marrakesh he turned to Mohammed and whispered: 'I smell *kief*. It would be a pity if I were to inform the French official who is sitting at the front of the bus. You and I, perhaps, could come to an arrangement.' Mohammed had to offer the man a share in his profit, and when they arrived in the city they set out together to find a dealer.

'The man to whom Mohammed usually sells his *kief* was away, and they were obliged to inquire for another. The person whom they asked demanded a further share. Then while they were walking through the market the sack fell open to reveal some of the leaves, and a passer-by helped them to rebundle it. So there were four people in the party when Mohammed finally sold his *kief*. He has made no profit.'

But Mohammed-ten-mules had salvaged *some* of his hashish money

When later we saw him he was looking much cleaner and more prosperous. He had bought himself a new *djellaba* and new shoes, and he had been shaved by one of the city barbers. While he was in Marrakesh he revisited the French doctor, who gave him some sort of injection for tuberculosis. He did not consider this sufficient, and on his return he employed his friends to burn a young tree so that he might inhale the smoke. This procedure was considered to be very effective in the treatment of coughs.

Talk of Mohammed ben Ahmed's visit to Marrakesh turned naturally to a discussion of the city itself, and our host regaled us with highly-coloured accounts of his several visits. Marrakesh to the Atlas tribesman has the same sort of attraction as has Southend to the Londoner: there are lights, gaiety and music. The delights of Marrakesh, however, are more exotic than those of an English holiday resort. Fully a quarter of the old city is occupied by brothels, and we wondered whether Mohammed ben Ahmed's tale of woe did not, for the benefit of his wife, cover less innocent expenditure. Certainly, if our host's accounts were true, there was plenty of opportunity for expensive licentiousness. Activities of this sort were the most important indulgences of people in the Ait Rbaa. There was very little hashish-smoking, although so much of the plant was grown, and the drinking of alcohol was practically unknown. Mohammed-one-mule told us, however, that the Jews in Telouet produced a powerful fig brandy, known as *mahia*. There were rumours, he said, that some of the Muslim inhabitants of the *kasbah*, including the Khalifa and the Caid, had developed a taste for it.

The story of the Jews in Morocco is an interesting one. They have been in the country for a very long time, and claim to have settled there after the fall of Jerusalem, or even earlier. There were certainly Jewish settlements in Morocco in Roman times, and since then their numbers have been reinforced by people expelled from various other countries, particularly from Spain. Quite often their physical features are indistinguishable from Berbers or Arabs, and they have adopted many of the local customs. Nevertheless they can be immediately recognized, at any rate in the country places, because they wear a small black skull-cap instead of the turban. The Berbers too wear skull-caps, but these are knitted in bright colours and geometrical designs.

Relations between the Jews and the other inhabitants of Morocco have usually been good, although of course racial intolerance *does* exist. In the old towns the Jews are strictly segregated into a special quarter or *mellah*. It is interesting to compare living conditions in a city between the *mellah* and the *medina*. The former is almost invariably dirtier and more squalid.

The Jews play an important part in Berber life. As money-lenders they help to stabilize the economy. The Berbers are notably improvident, and as soon as they have money, or indeed wealth in any form, tend to spend it quickly. Were it not for the money-lenders there might well be widespread starvation during the late winter and early spring. The Jews, too, have specialized in the practice of certain crafts. They are blacksmiths, tailors and carpenters, many of them itinerant.

Recently there has been a great emigration of Jews from Morocco to Israel; perhaps they felt unsafe in a Muslim country after the Arab-Israeli wars. But the departure of money-lenders and craftsmen has been a severe blow to many tribes in southern Morocco. They do not know how to keep accounts and forge iron, and there is no one now to do it for them.

Conversation at Mohammed's tea-party turned to the subject of our host himself. We were surprised to discover that he was the Mokkadem—the headman of Idirh—directly responsible to the Sheikh of the Ait Rbaa. Nevertheless he did not have as much influence in the village as the three rich men. We also discovered that he owned another house, as well as the one in which he lived, and that this house was empty. His father had owned a half-share, and Mohammed had bought the other half for 12,500 francs. Presumably, therefore, a two-roomed home in the Ait Rbaa costs £25. Mohammed offered to rent it to us. The usual custom, he said, was that no one from another village could live in Idirh without the permission of all its inhabitants. He would have to discover their feelings before the letting could be arranged. But there were no objections, and two weeks later he handed it over to us. The rent was a pair of trousers.

Afterwards members of the party oscillated between the camp and the house, and saw even less of each other.

About this time I paid a visit to Titullah, a few miles to the south of Idirh. One of its inhabitants, Sayid ben Brahim, had begged me to go there so that I could treat his wife. At five o'clock in the afternoon Sayid arrived to escort me to his home. We walked along a winding path by the side of the stream. I hailed many friends who were sitting above their fields, shouting and hurling stones to scare away the birds. I heard the sharp 'crack' of their slings and the whine of stones flying through the air. We climbed up slopes of black, cinder-like scree, crossed over another small stream, and passed through a grove of trees where crocuses grew.

When we arrived at Titullah we found the whole village awaiting us, and they followed in a long crocodile as we climbed the steep track between the houses. Titullah is higher than Idirh, and from the top of the village there was a marvellous view of the valley. The mountains were hazy in the soft evening light, and we could see cattle grazing in the green fields below. It was utterly peaceful.

This was the place that Joseph Thomson had described as 'a dreary solitude'.

We were joined by the *taleb* of Titullah—an opulent man in a shining white *djellaba*, who carried a beautifully embossed silver dagger. Sayid gave us tea in his little house, but the *taleb* was asked to prepare it. Then Sayid's wife came forward. A pale girl, she sat feeding her baby at the breast while I examined her. She seemed to be suffering from an infection of the sinuses. She complained of pains in the head, particularly when she bent down, and she had sensitive patches above the eyes, a cough, and a slight temperature. I gave her nose drops and penicillin snuff. Sayid gave me three boiled eggs.

The presence of the *taleb* was explained when he asked me to examine his child.

The *taleb's* house was the largest in the village, and very grand by local standards. It had great iron-studded oak doors, and a walled courtyard. Inside, the individual rooms also had doors, which were painted red and blue in geometrical designs. He showed us into a long whitewashed room, whose ceiling was covered with woven patterns of thick cane, alternating red and yellow. There were coloured tiles set in the window alcoves, and the windows themselves were protected by complicated wrought-iron grids. At one end of the room was a recess containing a pile of books, the first I had seen in the Ait Rbaa. It was clear that the *taleb* was a well-educated man. Over mint-tea he asked me about London. He would not believe me when I told him that it was twenty times the size of Casablanca.

'Casablanca is the biggest city in the world,' he said.

He asked if we had much water for irrigation in England, and then what were our relations with Egypt. The last was a difficult question to answer diplomatically, since I knew that he had read the Arabic newspapers, many of which are published in Egypt and are violently anti-British. I told him that our relations with the Egyptians were not good, because they had failed to honour their contracts.

After a meal of *kus kus* and mutton, which was well-prepared but 'sheep of the sacrifice' and therefore unpleasant, the child was brought in and a large audience assembled to watch my treatment. Among them was Mohammed ben Embark, the man who had refused to send his wife to the French doctor. The child had a badly infected eyelid which had swollen so as to close the eye completely. I told them to put hot, clean compresses on it, and gave an injection of penicillin.

After another round of mint-tea the *taleb* asked Mohammed ben Embark to escort us home. Mohammed was one of the finest looking men in the valley, broad, six feet tall, with a lean handsome face. He would have done well as a Hollywood Sheikh. I was disillusioned when he refused to go with us. He was, he said, afraid of the dark.

Sayid finally led us back to camp, but he too was obviously frightened. He walked ahead, holding an acetylene lamp at arm's length and singing nervously. He took us by a route over the mountains rather than the one by which we had come. It was a more open road, and there were fewer places where marauders could conceal themselves. We arrived safely and shared coffee with Sayid before turning in.

Each day more and more people appeared for treatment. They came now even from villages ten or fifteen miles away; our reputation had spread. A few of the visitors stand out in my memory. There was Lhassan ben Idirh's daughter, a pretty little girl who could not explain how she had received a terrible gash across her wrist because she was completely deaf and dumb. Then there was the village buffoon, Hassi ben Hamed, a young man with a brown turban, a torn white *djellaba*, and a wide grin. He claimed that his stomach enlarged enormously after meals. I gave him a good dose of castor oil. Another memorable patient was the man who had been shot in the stomach during rioting in Marrakesh. He had escaped from the French hospital, travelled by bus, then walked across the mountains to his village. Several days later he came to me for treatment. He strolled into the camp, pulled up his robe, and said:

'Please could you treat this?'

There was a hole in his stomach about the size of a penny where the bullet had entered, and another larger one in his back where it had left.

I poured penicillin into the hole, bound him up, and hoped for the best. I shall never understand how he survived, but he was still active when we left the Ait Rbaa.

As a result of the deluge of patients our medical supplies were running perilously short. I airmailed to England, to Imperial Chemical Industries and to British Drug Houses, explaining the situation. Both these firms very kindly flew out additional medicines free of charge.

Our relations with the villagers seemed to be continually improving. One afternoon we were told that a man had been caught stealing figs and would we come to the village to 'collect the goat'. A little mystified, we made our way up to the shack that served as a mosque, where a laughing crowd was gathered around a man who was carving up two carcasses. Hadj Lhassan was very obviously in charge of proceedings. The slaughterer was the thief who, having been caught in the act, was compelled to kill the goats and to divide them amongst all the households in the village. This fine was known as '*insof*'. By now we were considered part of the village and took our share. We were pleased, but did not enjoy the goat, which was indescribably tough.

The custom of *insof* demands some explanation. The undue power of the Khalifa and Sheikhs in the Glaoua tribe, or of the 'Council of Elders' in others, is checked by a system of blood feuds and by the formation of parties known as *sofs*. These parties are brought into being for trade, political, or other purposes. The term signifies a group whose members swear to render aid to each other in cases of necessity. Each *sof* may be allied with similar fraternities in neighbouring villages, and the ramifications of the organization can extend through entire districts. Within the village, members of each *sof* are united by the closest bonds, the obligations having a greater importance than any personal interests or even ties of kinship. Nevertheless, although loyal to the *sof* while he is a member of it, the Berber thinks little of transferring his allegiance from one *sof* to another if he thinks that he will gain thereby. The funds of the *sof* are raised by subscription from its members, and are administered by the heads of the organization (known as '*malinsofs*'), usually men of powerful families and private wealth, who may expend considerable sums on secret services without rendering account to the members.

One of the activities of the *sofs* ensures that the crops are harvested at the right time, so that the village derives the maximum benefit from them. An improvident farmer might, for instance, cut his corn early in order to earn quick money, even though by waiting he would get more. The *sofs* therefore decree that if a man harvests his crop before a certain date, he must pay a fine, or *insof*.

* * * *

Although we felt at home in the village, there were the inevitable petty irritations. On one occasion a delegation came down from Idirh.

'Please,' they asked, 'would you not excessively pay the blacksmith in Mohammed ben Ali's fields?' This was not the most intelligible of requests, but M'Barek explained that 'paying the blacksmith' was, for some reason, the local euphemism for going to the lavatory. We had been using a nearby field as a latrine, and its owner was offended. We explained that this activity would, no doubt, improve his crops. Nevertheless he preferred us to go elsewhere.

In order to soften the blow, the delegation invited us to tea. It was a merry party, and included all three Mohammeds, and Lhassan. While we were sitting down, Mohammed-one-mule tore the trousers which were under his *djellaba* and exposed himself in what the others considered to be an indecent fashion. Lhassan laughed and said:

'Mohammed will have to pay the *insof*.'

There were several claimants for the post of *malinsof* to receive the fine. Mohammed-one-mule refused to pay.

'The fault lies not with me, but with *M'soor Chef*, who has not yet paid me my rent.'

The accusation was true. I had not been able to get into Taddert to buy him the trousers which we had offered in exchange for the use of his house. It was finally decided that we should pay the fine if the trousers were not soon forthcoming. The business of the *insof* became a sort of joke between ourselves and the villagers. If anyone did something of which the others disapproved there would be a general cry of '*insof*'. It helped us out of a number of embarrassing situations.

Once we were entertaining Lhassan, Mohammed-one-mule, and Mohammed ben Ali. An open packet of cigarettes lay on one of the camp-beds, and Lhassan took a cigarette without first asking our permission. We all decided that this was a social misdemeanour worthy of the *insof*. A long and hilarious debate ensued, while we discussed what punishment would be suitable. Eventually, by general acclaim, we decided that Lhassan must eat cascara pills. The miscreant objected bitterly, saying that this was too grave a penalty, and fled from the

H

camp with the two Mohammeds in hot pursuit. But he was caught, and brought back struggling to the scene of the crime. The others held him down while I administered the purgative dose. Lhassan left us precipitately soon after, but he later maintained that the cascara had not affected him. No one believed it.

*   *   *   *

For the men of Idirh about the only break from the monotony of village life was a visit to the *souk* or village market. *Souks* are purely local affairs, but around the stone booths one could buy sugar, tea, dates and cotton clothes, and meet old friends. Humphrey and M'Barek left early one morning in the hour of diffused light before sunrise to go to the Thursday *souk* at Telouet. The first woman passed them with her jar going to fetch water at the spring; an old man was shaking out a rug on the roof of his house; a younger man came striding out of the village with an adze to look at his irrigation ditches, since it would be his turn to have the water when the evening came.

They made a detour to swing round the mountain-tops and passed a shepherds' encampment with its cluster of tiny stone shacks. Women were strolling round the camp, their babies in their arms, chatting to their neighbours like gypsies with all the time in the world on their hands. It was nearing midday as they dropped down to the market, and a scorching wind was blowing dust across the gravelled plain, making it oppressive to walk. A two-way stream of traffic passed to and from the *souk*. Men were coming away on their mules clutching chickens and sacks, a child or two on the animal's back, and flouncing wives in yellow dresses astride behind them. Old men sat heaped on the haunches of long-suffering donkeys, their toes almost dragging in the dust. Others were hurrying on foot to the *souk* before it closed.

Within the circle of booths there was a colourful crowd jostling round the merchants, arguing out the prices and greeting acquaintances. In the quieter corners where there was shade and where water could be boiled, little groups of men gossiped over tea. Humphrey and M'Barek made their purchases and found a friend with a mule to take them back to Idirh. Then they sat down wearily in the shade of a tree to rest until the day was cooler.

Soon the market had dispersed; there was only a group of black-capped Jews sitting cross-legged in a circle to sort out the morning's takings, and a single Berber dozing beside a basket of grapes.

It was late in the day when they stood at the top of the pass. To the south the great trade route had once passed through the lower mountains, and on to the palm-flanked river of the Draa that swept south and was lost to sight in the desert. Then, passing isolated man-made wells, the caravans had made their way across the Sahara to Timbuctoo. It was on this route through the mountains that the Sultan Abou Abbas Ahmed el-Mansour must have sent his army of 8,000 mules, 5,600 men, cavalry and cannon to cross the Sahara in 1590, and to seize the gold of the great Songhai kingdom in the western Sudan. The armies of more recent Sultans had also passed this way to collect their taxes from the rebellious tribes of the *bled-siba*. But little of the route remains beyond the broken mule-track—a stumbling, staggering track through rocks and boulders. Behind Telouet, in the full light of the setting sun, Humphrey and M'Barek saw the strange reddish-yellow eroded mountains, like sand-castles washed by the sea. To the north, the valley of the Ait Rbaa was indistinct in a hazy glare. Down at the bottom, some two thousand feet below the pass, lay the villages, hidden in the shade of the mountains.

*   *   *   *

Humphrey moved about a good deal more than the rest of us. He made several other journeys including two to the north, when he visited Zerekten, a village about ten miles down the valley from Idirh. On his second visit he stayed there for several days, taking a mule so that he could bring back specimens of the pottery produced nearby.

His path from Idirh to Zerekten lay for the whole of its length alongside the stream of the Ait Rbaa. It followed the old caravan route, and it was easy to see that this had once been a prosperous road. The track was wide, and in many places it had been built up with stones to provide a good walking surface for the caravans. About five miles from Idirh he came to the 'coloured mountain'—a great piece of rock that jutted out into the valley. It contained manganese ore, laid down in horizontal strata of alternating purple and green. During the day the mountain looked very much like any other, for the bright sun bleached it. But in the softer evening light the whole mass glowed with intense colour, like an enormous Neapolitan ice-cream.

Nearer Zerekten the mountain sides became progressively steeper until the valley was almost a canyon. Zerekten was a mud village larger than Idirh, and it boasted a weekly *souk* that attracted tribesmen

from many of the surrounding settlements. The Sheikh of the area, Si
Hassan, was a rich man related to the Khalifa at Telouet, and he had
been much influenced by the European way of life. He dressed himself
in French clothes, and he had built a track from the main road to his
kasbah so that he could reach it in his large American motor-car. He
had done a good deal to modernize the interior of his castle, but not to
the extent of improving sanitation; nor, it seemed, to removing para-
sites; for it was here, and here only, that members of our party had
trouble with bed-bugs.

A few miles to the east of Zerekten, in the valley of a tributary of
the Ait Rbaa, lived a community of potters. Humphrey spent two
days with them, learning the secrets of their craft and collecting samples
of their clays and glazes. Their repertoire of products was not great,
and little effort was made to decorate the plain earthenware pots, the
heavy water-jars, and the small glazed dishes. All of them were baked
in a red clay, and the glaze used was *galena*, a lead ore which occurred
in the surrounding hills. They applied it directly to the pots, unmixed
with any other substance, before refiring them. Humphrey has since
discovered that this is a very unusual technique and of considerable
interest to pottery experts.

The community of potters, unlike the other villages in the region,
was still administered by an *Ait Arba'in*, or 'Council of Elders', elected
by the villagers. There were no Sheikhs or Mokkadems. It was the
traditional system of Berber government, by which the tribes ruled
themselves before the Glaoui family's rise to power. Perhaps this remote village was not of sufficient importance to be required to change
its administration. The words *Ait Arba'in* mean, 'The People of the
Forty'. Presumably the council of elders traditionally had forty
members. In this village, however, there were only eight, and Humphrey was entertained by each of them in succession. He returned
very well fed.

*   *   *   *

Although Humphrey was our busiest traveller, the rest of us did
from time to time make excursions into the surrounding countryside.
John, Peter and I explored a valley which ran to the east of the Ait
Rbaa and parallel to it. In order to gain access to this valley we trekked
northwards as far as the 'Coloured Mountain', and then turned east
through a narrow canyon whose bed was filled with tamarisk bushes.

Some distance along it we came to a fresh mountain pool. By this time we were hot and tired, and we stripped off our clothes to splash about in the clear waters. We were surprised in our nakedness by the sudden arrival of a shepherd with his flock, and for decency's sake we were obliged to sit in the water up to our necks. The stream was very cold, and by the time the last sheep had ambled past we were blue and uncomfortable.

As we continued on our way we heard the voices of other shepherds shouting to each other from slope to slope. The shouting was pitched high, so that the sound would carry across the mountains. It sounded almost like a yodel. This form of communication enabled the tribesmen to pass information over great distances in a very short time, and if ever we made a journey the villages ahead of us knew of our coming hours before our actual arrival. The relatives of the Berbers, who once inhabited the Canary Islands—a people known as the Guanches—had developed to an even greater extent the art of communication across great distances. They whistled to each other, and these whistles had been refined into a complete language. Their descendants of today, who no longer speak Berber, have preserved the whistling language, but now they whistle in Spanish!

The valley was higher and narrower than the Ait Rbaa, and in the absence of human beings it was still covered with dense forests of oak. They had not been cut for firewood, nor had they been much damaged by the activities of the voracious Atlas goats. It is the goats which are steadily turning the region into a desert. One finds them chewing at every available piece of green vegetation; they are even known to climb trees in order to get at the leaves. But here there were large stretches of dark woodland through which scuttled great green lizards and little ground squirrels. Iridescent dragonflies zoomed between the trees, and pigeons fluttered in the higher branches.

John and I decided to return to the Ait Rbaa by climbing the ridge which separated us from it. Peter took the lowland route. It would be a race to see who got home first. John set a rattling pace, for he was far more used to mountaineering than I. It was not long before he had left me far behind as we scrambled up the near-vertical slopes. He waited at the top of the ridge—waited a considerable time. But when I got there I decided that the effort was worth it. There was a magnificent view of the valley spread out 2,000 feet below us.

Nevertheless I was concerned how we were to get down, for the far side was even steeper than the one we had climbed, and it was covered by long slopes of scree which seemed to end in vertical cliffs. We had to run diagonally across the scree—a frightening business, because as soon as we paused for breath we immediately started to slide down towards the cliff edge. Eventually, with relief, we found a piece of solid ground down which we could scramble, but by this time the soles of my shoes had been cut to ribbons on the sharp rocks, and I descended the last third of the slope virtually barefoot. It was very uncomfortable, and forced me to travel slowly, hopping carefully from rock to rock. We lost the race with Peter, and I spent the next few days in camp.

CHAPTER EIGHT

Alarms and Excursions

They cannot scare me with their empty spaces, . . .
I have it in me so much nearer home
To scare myself with my own desert places.

ROBERT FROST

O N 17 August, Charles Pasternak arrived at Idirh, with two mules carrying his equipment. He told us news of happenings in the north. The Nationalist party, it seemed, was increasing in strength, and there were more and more 'events', shooting, bomb-throwing, and the burning of tobacconists' shops.

The production of cigarettes in Morocco was a French Government monopoly, and the extreme nationalists had therefore decreed that no Moroccan should smoke. Terrorist gangs would order tobacconists to close down their shops, and if they refused they would be murdered and their premises would be sacked. On one occasion I remember publicly offering a cigarette to a Moroccan while we were standing in the *medina* at Rabat. I have never seen a man look so frightened.

'No, no,' he said, 'I cannot accept it here.'

He led me down a small alleyway and, under cover of my coat, I passed him the offending object. He concealed it for later use.

Charles told us that there were many rumours in the market-places about what would happen on 20 August, the anniversary of the deposition of Sultan Sidi Mohammed ben Youssef. It was whispered that Morocco would rise against the French, that all Europeans would be massacred, that communications would be cut and that the country would declare its independence. The French were prepared for trouble. Troops were being moved to strategic points, and Europeans evacuated from the *medinas*. In the Ait Rbaa the tribesmen were being pressed into the service of the Pasha to act as policemen in Marrakesh. They did not relish the prospect.

Before leaving Telouet the Khalifa had given Charles permission to take blood samples, but said that he must also have the approval of the French authorities in Ouazazate. Humphrey and Charles set off, taking with them Mohammed, Charles's interpreter, who was a college companion of M'Barek. In the desert town they visited a French Colonel, who absolutely refused to allow Charles to do his work. It was not permitted, he said, for people without medical qualifications to practise medicine upon the tribesmen. In vain did Charles point out that the taking of blood samples was not 'practising medicine'. He determined to go to Rabat, and to get permission from the central French Government. Humphrey returned to Idirh.

The fateful day passed peacefully in the valley. It was like any other day. A week later we had still heard no news from the north, for the road from Taddert to Marrakesh was closed and no traffic came across the mountains. The *patron's* telephone line had been cut; there were neither newspapers nor mail. Then some of the men who had been serving as the Pasha's policemen began to filter back into the valley. They had horrifying stories to tell. The *medina* at Marrakesh, they said, was still surrounded by French troops, and aeroplanes were bombing the interior. There were rumours of bloodshed in all the major cities of the country.

Among the returning villagers was the son of Boghrib, a dashing young man in a blue cloak, who was a *mohasni* in the service of Si Sadek. He knew Abdullah, and had seen Humphrey and Peter when they visited the Palace. He came down one evening to the camp, and we talked about the situation in Morocco.

'I joined the Pasha's guard,' he said, 'because I wanted to live in Marrakesh. The people here are uncivilized. But now that the Pasha supports the French against the rest of Morocco I am no longer happy to serve him, for I do not like the French. It is difficult for the Glaoua; we are faithful to the Pasha because he is one of our tribe, but we cannot agree with his actions. If you had been French we would have burnt your camp to the ground.'

I asked him why he disliked them so much.

'We Moroccans cannot get promotion or education. We are not allowed to travel freely. The French are bombing Marrakesh and killing my countrymen. Is this not enough?'

He said that if the Pasha would let them, the Glaoua could drive the French from Morocco.

'We are not afraid of war, but the *nasrani* are cowards.'

I was irritated that he used the word *nasrani* (Christians), which includes all Europeans.

At about this time Charles returned from Rabat. He had been given permission to do his work on blood groups under medical supervision in the hospital at Ouazazate. He stayed with us for only a brief time before continuing on his way to the desert, but he was able to give us a true account of the situation in the north. There had indeed been riots in every large Moroccan town. In two small French settlements, Oued Zem and Khouribga, a large part of the European population had been massacred. A whole tribe had swept down from the mountains to attack Oued Zem. The town had been taken completely unprepared. People were murdered in their homes. A doctor was cut down among his patients in the hospital.

Charles hitch-hiked back from Rabat, and was picked up by a couple in a small car. The woman was weeping. She had just lost her daughter at Oued Zem. The girl had been preparing to go out, when a gang of men broke into the house, chopped off her head with a hatchet, and killed her children. Her husband returned to find them all horribly mutilated.

Charles had been given another lift; in a car which drove along at high speed, shotguns trained out of the windows; the owner of the car was angry.

'What we need in this country is more soldiers. Then we could teach the bastards a lesson.'

On great stretches of his route the telegraph poles had been cut down. The *gueliz* in Marrakesh was deserted, the cafés were closed, the *medina* was indeed still surrounded by troops. But Charles said that the only bombs being dropped were of tear-gas.

These events seemed at first sight to have little effect upon our life in the village, but I began to suspect that there were undercurrents of hostility towards us. My suspicions started on a second visit to Tituallah, when my host took me aside: 'Do not,' he said, 'lend your guns to Boghrib's *mohasni*. There might be an accident.'

Some time later, one of our friends in the village told us that the *mohasni* had been suggesting that we were there for secret reasons of our own.

'Europeans are all the same,' he had said. 'They only do things for you in order to get something in return.'

I understand that the villagers had protested at this, and that he had said to them:

'Go to the English and ask them for something which you desire. See whether it will be given to you.' Suddenly we had demands for our cooking-pots, our camp-beds, our clothes. Of course we could not give them all away.

The *mohasni* became a regular visitor to the camp, but his manners did not improve. On one occasion he asked me for a cigarette, which I gave him. I saw him break it in two. Then he said: 'You have given me a broken one. May I have another?'

I debated with myself whether to have him thrown out of the camp, but discretion prevailed and he got his second cigarette. He made a number of demands that we should lend him our shotguns, demands which I steadfastly refused. A friend of the *mohasni* enquired: 'Is it not true that if something happened to you, there would be a war between England and France?' Needless to say, I denied it.

From this time on we heard many more outspoken criticisms of the French and the Pasha. It was now clear that el-Glaoui's power was waning, and it was reported that the Nationalists had gained control in a number of his tribes. They were supposed to have 'cells' infiltrating the tribal structure—an arrangement somewhat similar to Communist systems. The *sofs* would provide a very satisfactory frame-work on which to build such an organization, and I remembered that the *malinsofs* were often rich men in the villages. It seemed significant that the *mohasni* was a son of Boghrib.

It was from the *mohasni* that we first heard of a forthcoming celebration. This was known as the 'Water Feast' and on the morning of that day villagers visited each other to pour water over the heads of their friends. This was supposed to wash away grievances and quarrels. The evening was given over to singing and dancing. The *mohasni* invited us to come to the performance. A number of our friends were against our doing so, and came to the camp in order to dissuade us. It was not seemly, they said, for Europeans to be at a religious celebration of this sort. Lhassan ben Idirh and Mohammed-one-mule were the prime movers in this campaign. But we persuaded Lhassan to change his mind. He had for some time coveted our transparent polythene bags, and Humphrey offered to give him one if he would not raise an objection to our attending the feast. But Lhassan, at first, was adamant. Then I had an inspiration.

'Lhassan,' I said, 'you may have this present, whatever your feelings about the Water Feast.'

Immediately he replied, 'Thank you, M'soor Chef. Of course I shall raise no objection to your coming.'

He was not willing to be bribed, but he could be persuaded with a gift.

We entertained Mohammed ben Hamed and Mohammed ben Ali to dinner on the night of the feast, and the stars were bright as we climbed up to the village. Mohammed-one-mule held a sputtering lantern as he led the way along the narrow path. From the village drifted the sound of chanting voices and the strange accentuated rhythm of drums.

'The *ahouash* (dance) has begun', he said.

He took us to a square open space in the centre of the village. Dark figures huddled round its edges, family groups chattered, children ran hither and thither. In the middle of the square a wood fire blazed, casting grotesque shadows on the stone walls of the surrounding houses. Women sat on the roofs, silhouetted against the night sky.

Six men stood in a line before the fire. Each held a large leather tambour, and struck it in a slow rhythm—three beats, then a pause—repeated continuously. A young man began to sing. Soon others joined in, and the tempo increased. The song rose and fell. The singers began to sway and move their feet in time to the music—one pace forward, one pace back, and one to the side. From time to time a performer detached himself to tune his tambour over the fire. The singing grew to a tumult—then ended abruptly. Other songs followed, the number of performers growing as spectators joined in. They now formed themselves into two lines facing each other, with a sort of 'master of ceremonies' standing between them, and beating a counter-rhythm with his tambour. The whole group slowly rotated, swaying together from side to side.

The women on the roof-tops encouraged them with wild ululations. The strange cries of Berber women were famous in very ancient times. Herodotus, four hundred years before Christ, observed:

'. . . I think, too, that the crying of women at religious ceremonies also originated in Libya—for the Libyan women are much addicted to this practice, and they do it very beautifully. . . .'

But I cannot concur with Herodotus in his appreciation of the sound; it is positively blood-curdling.

As the evening wore on, the songs became more vigorous, and the rhythm yet faster. Religious music had started the performance, but now they sang of love.

The love songs were hard to recognize, for they were couched in strange similes: 'If a man has a beautiful field of mint,' they chanted, 'he must guard it well.' Some of the other songs were less delicately phrased. The entertainment became more rowdy. Hassi ben Hamed, the village buffoon, jumped into the firelight and shouted out what was clearly the Moroccan equivalent of a barrack-room ballad. There were gusts of laughter. Then an old man came forward to perform a very effective mime of loading and firing an ancient rifle. While I was watching him, I felt a tug at my coat. It was Hassi ben Hamed, his face pale in the wavering light. He pulled urgently at my arm.

'*Ilf*,' he said, '*ilf, ilf*.'

I did not understand what he was trying to say. '*Ilf*' is the Berber word for the wild boar.

M'Barek was not with us to interpret, for he had excused himself from the feast, saying that he felt unwell. I thought that perhaps Hassi wished to hunt the boar, so I pointed questioningly towards the mountains. But he said, 'No, no,' repeated the word '*ilf*' and pointed directly at me. Then he made a sound like a gun firing, and waved his hand in the direction of the roof-top opposite. The women had departed, and in their place there were other figures looking down into the square. Some of them had staves—or were they rifles?

I have already mentioned my tendency to imagine dangers that do not exist. Suddenly I had the thought that this was the day in the village on which unpleasantnesses were removed. Could it be that they intended to remove us? I had a vision of the men on the opposite roof waiting to shoot us down as we watched the performance, to shoot us down like wild boar at bay. This was an Eastern method of arranging such things. You invited your guests to a feast, and then murdered them. I noticed that the children had departed, and that the remainder of the spectators were lined up below the opposite wall. The *mohasni* now seemed to be in charge of the ceremony. Only the two Mohammeds remained with us, and Mohammed ben Ali sat between us and the villagers, dandling his youngest child on his knee. Here, I thought, is the true friend, protecting us from the plot of the *mohasni*.

The whole thing was ridiculous, but at that moment all the circumstances of the past week: the enquiries about our guns, the reluctance of our friends to let us come to the feast, seemed to fit together into a complete picture. For a short time, before I managed to get control of myself, I was very frightened. But we stayed until late in the evening, and returned without incident to camp.

I cannot have been very good at concealing my fears, for on the following day a delegation came down from the village.

'Last night at the feast,' they said, 'Hassi ben Hamed offended you in some way. We could see that this was so.'

I stoutly maintained that it was of no importance. 'Nevertheless,' they said, 'it will not recur. He has been sent into the mountains to tend sheep.'

We did not see him again.

*   *   *   *

One evening, Sayid ben Brahim came from Titullah to say that his wife was much better, and no longer 'in bed'. He then went on to warn us that this was the time of year for floods.

'If it rains in the mountains for more than a day,' he said, 'a great wall of water sweeps down through the valley. It happens very quickly.'

He positively begged us not to stay at the present camp site.

We pondered this warning, and went for a second opinion to Idirh. 'Certainly it happens,' they said. 'But we know in advance. We will warn you when there is danger of floods. But of course if it is the will of God that you should drown, there is nothing we can do about it.'

With this pious thought to encourage us, we remained under the walnut tree.

*   *   *   *

Some days later I left camp for Marrakesh to see the French authorities. I hoped to learn more about the political situation, and to inform them of our plans. Furthermore, Colin and Thesiger were now overdue, and I was worried about them. We had not heard from them since before the events of the twentieth. At about that time, if their journey went according to plan, they should have arrived among the Smalla, the tribe which descended on Oued Zem.

I left the camp at about 5 p.m., and climbed the steep path to Taddert. At first it was bare rock, but higher up there were scattered scrubby oaks, then the path crossed patches of scree, where I had to run in order to prevent myself from sliding down the slopes.

I had been climbing for some time when I met two men, armed with clubs, who were sitting in the shade of a little oak tree. I greeted them with the usual *salaams*, but they did not reply. This worried me, for I remembered Thesiger telling us that, in Mohammedan countries, one could always assess people's intentions; those who wished you ill would never reply to a greeting.

'But perhaps,' I thought, 'it is merely that they do not wish to give the blessing of God to an infidel.'

I continued up the path, and a little while later was disturbed to find that they were plodding silently behind me. Not a word was said as we walked in a crocodile to the top of the pass. I was becoming really frightened. Then, to my relief, I met a mule caravan coming in the opposite direction. The man leading it was a friend of mine, and I greeted him with pleasure; indeed, I was positively effusive. My two 'companions' faded from sight, and I did not see them again on the journey.

Below the pass the road continued along a dry stream-bed. I was hurrying to avoid another encounter with the men, and hoping to reach Taddert before nightfall, and I did not look where I was going. Suddenly there was a hiss, and an enormous snake writhed away from the path into some bushes. I had missed treading on it by a mere six inches. I do not know if the snake was poisonous, but it was well over four feet long. The evening was an eventful one; later I met a great crested lizard, about as long as the snake.

I arrived at the *auberge* in less than two hours. This was a record for the journey, but as John commented later, I had the hounds of hell behind me. I drank four bottles of Coca-cola in quick succession, and left notes for Colin, in case he should arrive while I was away, and for Charles, who was soon due back from Ouazazate. Early the following morning I boarded the bus to Marrakesh.

We arrived in the city just before midday. It was Sunday and all the offices of the French Administration were closed, so I wandered into the great square of the Djemaa el Fna. This time it was back to normal, crowded with little booths and noisy with the clamours of massed humanity. I came to the Djemaa el Fna, as most of its visitors had come, from the unsophisticated life of the mountains. I viewed it, that day, almost through the eyes of a tribesman. It seemed incredibly busy, incredibly civilized, and there was excitement everywhere. At one stall a smooth-tongued and quick-fingered gentleman was extracting money from innocent bystanders with a variant of 'spot the card'. A story-teller nearby held his audience enthralled, his voice rising and falling with the drama of the tale. A little further on a row of veiled women were slapping circular loaves of bread to show that they were light and well-baked. Musicians played at one corner of the square, their drums beating a complicated rhythm—accentuating the strangeness of the scene. Water-carriers strolled through the crowd ringing their harsh bells.

I sat down on the terrace of the Café de France to watch the colourful throng, and I noticed another European, also watching. Although he was dressed in sun-glasses and a highly-coloured shirt, I decided that he was English. Perhaps it was a certain aloofness in his bearing which betrayed him. I approached him and asked if my guess was correct. He nodded assent, and offered me a drink.

He lived, I discovered, in the *medina*. He and a few of his friends had refused to go when the French ordered the evacuation of Europeans. This was the more remarkable since some months previously he had been very seriously injured, when a bomb was thrown on to the terrace of the café. He had been sitting then where he was sitting now. But, he said, he felt at home in Marrakesh, and he was not willing to allow mere politics (or, it seemed, bombs) to interfere with his existence. He invited me to luncheon at his home, which lay in the heart of the *medina*, among the *souks*. We wandered through narrow streets, past little shops selling leather-work and jewellery and carpets. The *souks* were crowded, but there was not a European to be seen, and I felt uncomfortable, sensing the hostility of passers-by. I remembered that a Frenchman had once said:

'Here they hate us, even with their eyes.'

My friend's house was typical of those in the *medina*. From the exterior I saw only a plain blank white-washed wall and a heavy wooden door. But once inside I found myself in a little square patio which was paved with colourful tiles, and open to the sky. At the centre was a pool where a fountain played. Rooms opened out in all directions from the patio, and I was surprised to find that all but one were completely empty of furniture. The exception contained a single brass bedstead.

My host explained. He had been working at one of the American air bases, directing Moroccan personnel on a construction job. The task had been completed, and now he was unemployed. In order to remain in Marrakesh he had sold all his furniture. I wondered what other city in the world could have such a fascination for a man that he would risk his life and sell his belongings in order to remain there.

We ate our luncheon squatting on the bare tiles.

In the afternoon we strolled back through the *souks* towards the Djemaa el Fna, and I felt once more the hard stare of unfriendly eyes. Several Arabs spat upon the ground as we passed. It was a strange, sad state of affairs. These men did not know us. They hated us only because our skins were white, because to them we represented a system they despised. In a neutral place we might have been their friends, but here we were isolated by barriers of ignorance and prejudice.

I had a senseless desire to expostulate, to say:

'Judge me if you must, but for God's sake judge me as a person— not as a political abstraction.'

But it was no use.

Then, while I was thinking these things, a voice boomed out of the crowd.

'M'soor Chef, M'soor Chef. Salaam-o-alikum.'

A blue-coated figure ran forward—it was Sayid ben Brahim from Titullah. He grinned as we exchanged enthusiastic compliments, and suddenly the narrow streets seemed less hostile. Even here one could find a friend, even here the barriers could be broken.

A short time later I was greeted by another man from the valley. My host was impressed.

'You seem to be well-known in these parts,' he said. I felt ridiculously pleased with myself.

*   *   *   *

We sat once again in the café overlooking the Djemaa el Fna. A magazine salesman had set up his stall nearby, and a crowd was gathering around it. There seemed to be more than the usual interest. The stall, we discovered, was selling the latest edition of a Paris magazine which featured photographs of the massacre at Oued Zem. In the true traditions of French journalism the pictures were gruesome, sparing the reader no unpleasant detail.

Each Moroccan who bought a copy was immediately surrounded by an eager group of his countrymen, reading over his shoulder—and chuckling delightedly at the terrible pictures. There seemed to be hundreds of people laughing. At that moment I came very near to hating the Moors—for it was one of the most horrifying things I have ever seen. But the faults were not all on their side. I remembered the fat hunter of frogs taking photographs at Taddert, the arrogant jack-

booted French soldiers, the *colons* who brandished guns and talked of
'shooting the bastards down'.

It was not possible to lay the blame for events in Morocco on one
party or another. It was not fair to say, as newspapers and politicians
were so fond of saying, 'French imperialism was at fault'; or. 'The
trouble was caused by paid agitators from Cairo.'

If I had been an Arab, I would have behaved as the Arabs did—I
would probably have thrown bombs. Had I been a Frenchman, I
would have fought to defend my property and the interests of my
country. As an outsider, an observer, I could only marvel and regret the
tragedy; a tragedy made the more poignant because it was inevitable.
The Protectorate had within it the seeds of its own destruction, and the
resulting conflict could not conveniently be summed up in terms of
black and white, of good and bad. In the darkness, 'all the cats were
grey'.

*   *   *   *

That evening we met two Americans who, like my host, had refused
to leave the *medina*. One of them, an archaeologist, had spent a year at
New College, and he invited me to stay at his home. He wanted to
hear the latest news of Oxford.

At this time there was a curfew in Marrakesh, and at seven o'clock
precisely the Djemaa el Fna was completely cleared of people. Soldiers
patrolled the streets throughout the night. At 6.45 the archaeologist led
me to his house. This one was furnished, and tastefully decorated with
fine examples of Moroccan crafts. Keys, silver daggers and powder-
horns hung from the walls. There were electric lamps fashioned from
great water-jars, and good tribal carpets on the floors.

It was pleasant to sleep, for the first time in many weeks, on a bed
with mattress and sheets; but I was unused to it, and several times
during the night I crept out of my room, to sit in one of the cane
chairs on the patio and watch the stars wheeling above the restless city.
There were distant sounds, snatches of Arab music, and, once, faint
shouting and the rattle of shots.

The next morning I visited Lieutenant G. at the Contrôle Civil. He
was in a cheerful mood.

'There won't be any more trouble here. The French will not quarrel
with the Pasha.'

I wondered if the power of el-Glaoui would be of service to them

I

much longer. I asked him what would happen to the present Sultan. Popular feeling now seemed to be solidly against him.

'I think he will "take a holiday". A Regency Council is being considered, but Sidi Mohammed ben Youssef will not return.'

I told him that Colin and Thesiger were overdue. He was concerned, and promised to make inquiries.

But his inquiries were not necessary. I visited the *Gueliz* that afternoon, to pick up a parcel of medicines from England, and there I met Charles Pasternak. He had just come from Taddert, and he told me the cheering news that Colin and Thesiger had arrived at Idirh on the morning after my departure.

Charles and I decided to put up for the night at a small hotel on the fringes of the Djemaa el Fna, but before retiring we determined to see the *medina* when it was empty—after the curfew.

The 'concourse of sinners' was no longer aptly named. It lay pale and deserted in the moonlight, and the only manifestations of life were the ringing footsteps of soldiers on patrol. They might have been good men—those soldiers.

The little streets were similarly barren, but they were dark—and vaguely sinister. What was hidden behind those faceless walls? Were there figures in that doorway across the dead street?

Charles led me to a place which he knew; where, he said, we could get food. We banged on a shuttered gate—to be admitted into a little courtyard, a courtyard which had been originally a Moroccan patio, but which was now transformed. Along one wall ran a series of cages, with canaries and budgerigars chattering and chirruping. Another was hung with long gaudy posters of bullfights.

We had come to the home of a Spanish family, and we shared their evening meal in a chaos of dogs and birds and children. They gave us soup, poached eggs and aubergines, grilled sardines and tomato, wine and fruit. The bill came to less than four shillings.

We returned to bed through the dark alleys of Marrakesh.

*　　*　　*　　*

Lieutenant G., the next morning at the Contrôle Civil, was relieved to hear that our two travellers had come safely home. He seemed less pleased when I told him about our plans for the future, but eventually he agreed that we could go south into the desert.

Charles was not coming with us. Although we had seen little of him, he was obliged to return to Oxford, where he was doing post-graduate research; research students do not have long holidays. I saw him off on his way back to England.

Two days later I rose at 4 a.m. to catch the bus for Ait Ourir. It was due to leave at five, but did not appear at the bus-station until 7.30. None of the passengers seemed to mind the delay; they merely lay down on the road, pulled the hoods of the *djellabas* over their heads, and went back to sleep. The loading of luggage, chickens and a small goat on the roof of the bus took half an hour. We left Marrakesh at eight.

The road led round the walls of the *medina*, and once again I saw hundreds of sheep, mules, camels and men moving on their way to and from the city. The lines of figures cast long shadows in the hazy morning light, and the palm heads hung motionless above them, but it was the turreted red ramparts of the city that dominated the scene.

Further along the road we passed a convoy of troop-carriers—heading south.

I disembarked at the *cantine* of Ait Ourir and the proprietor kindly drove me to the Contrôle Civil, where I visited the French doctor. He had a neat little hospital next to the Post, and he was busy with a queue of patients when I was shown in. He did not know the whereabouts of the Ait Rbaa, so I told him of the valley, and suggested that he come with me to treat the villagers.

'I cannot treat people, unless they come to me,' he said. 'I have too many patients even here.'

But he gave me some more medicines, particularly aureomycin for the treatment of trachoma. (This was a set-back for M'Barek, who had said: 'You will get no medicines from the French; they are far too mean.')

There was not a bus to Taddert until the following day, so I decided to see if I could get a lift. While I was waiting on the road, a Moor came up, riding a very expensive-looking bicycle, and asked for money. Clearly I was still near civilization.

The first car to come along the road was a large Cadillac, and it stopped to pick me up. The driver was Director of the mines at Imini, and he told me that they produced some of the purest manganese ore in the world. The aerial railway had been built to carry this ore across the mountains, but it was, he said, very susceptible to sabotage, and the cable was continually being cut. When this happened the ore had to be

transported by road across the Tizi-n-Tishka pass—a very expensive
proceeding.

'Morocco is rich in minerals,' he said, 'but most of them haven't
been exploited. There's oil in the north, and the wells already supply
half Morocco's needs. We're looking for oil also in the Sahara, but so
far we haven't found any. There's iron ore at Tindouf, cobalt at Bou
Azzer, and asbestos in many parts of the Atlas.'

I asked him if there had been any disturbance in the mines.

'We had a bit of trouble, not too much; but one never knows with
these people. They'll be friendly with you one minute, and then—
pouf—they'll stab you in the back.'

He dropped me at Taddert, and by four in the afternoon I was back
at Idirh. Colin and Thesiger were there, and they told me about their
journey. It had been an exciting one.

I cannot tell the full story of their remarkable walk. A second-
hand version would not do it justice, and I hope he will write his own
account of the trip.

Colin and Thesiger left Telouet on 2 August, and with a guide and
a single mule they struck east from the kasbah to the lake of Tamda.
They took no food, nor did they have to buy any, for wherever they
went they were hospitably entertained by the tribesmen.

The first part of their journey took them along the southern slopes of
the Atlas, yellow and red hills completely bare of vegetation. They
spent the nights in the mud-built castles of sheikhs and rich merchants.
They circled the great mountain mass of the Irhil Mgoun, then followed
one of its streams south to El Kelaa, which they reached on the eighth
day. There they were entertained by the Khalifa, who drove them to
the market town of Boumalne on the following morning.

Boumalne is one of the most important trading centres of the
northern Sahara, and in its souks one can buy tea trays from Birming-
ham, cosmetics from New York, bon-bons from Paris, a goatskin with
the gory head still attached, or a charm to cure headache.

Boumalne lies at the point where the River Dades issues from its
mountain gorges into the flat desert. The gorges of the Dades are
among the most inspiring sights in Morocco, and the scenery rivals,
and resembles, that of the Grand Canyon. Over a vast period of time
the river has cut an enormous trough in the pale rock. The sides of the
gorges are bare, but there is a ribbon of green vegetation alongside the
river.

The two travellers journeyed along the Dades until they reached M'Semrir, near its source. Here they met Mr and Mrs Ernest Gellner, the anthropologists of London University whom we had first encountered in Rabat. They were studying the tribes of the region, and had their base at Zaouia Ahansal on the north side of the range. Colin and Thesiger joined the Gellners on a visit to the Abdi plateau, an enormous expanse of limestone pavement about nine thousand feet above sea-level, where nomadic tribes graze their cattle. The party spent several days on the plateau, enjoying the hospitality of the black nomad tents, before they descended the steep cliffs which surround it to Zaouia Ahansal. Colin and Thesiger remained in Zaouia Ahansal rather longer than they had intended, for they were cut off for several days by torrential floods, which swept suddenly down from the hills to demolish bridges and fords. The two travellers finally got back to Idirh after an absence of five weeks.

CHAPTER NINE

Never to Dream

Over the pass the voices one by one
Faded, and the hill slept.

NEWBOLT

AFTER Colin and Thesiger had come back from their journey, and I had returned from Marrakesh, the party settled down once more to the routine of life in camp. The villagers were impressed by Thesiger. He was more severe with them than we had ever been, and they concluded that he was an English Pasha. He even succeeded in intimidating the *mohasni*. Colin also created a stir, for by now he had a luxuriant growth of beard. He became known as 'the hairy one'.

Humphrey lived almost entirely at the house in the village, and the rest of us found it difficult to understand how he managed to survive, for the two rooms were ill-ventilated and stiflingly hot. The mud floor contained liberal proportions of dung, and the atmosphere, to say the the least of it, was aromatic. Chickens and other less pleasant forms of life wandered in and out at all times of the day and night. But Humphrey found the house useful. Living in it he felt part of the community, and perhaps the community itself accepted him more readily. Although in general his investigations went well, there was one matter which caused him difficulty. He tried to persuade the villagers to disclose the ownership of the fields. But they were reluctant to do so, and perhaps they still had suspicions that we were connected in some way with the administration, and that we might pass on such details for the purposes of taxation. Eventually, however, Humphrey managed to persuade Lhassan and Boghrib to show him their fields, and he was at any rate able to map out the possessions of one poor and one rich man. He also studied the few handicrafts that were practised in the village.

The women used a primitive form of loom on which they wove woollen cloaks and blankets, of simple design and coarse texture. Although the Glaoua tribe in some places produces very fine black and white carpets, we did not find anyone in Idirh who did so. The blankets, however, were sufficiently heavy to be used as floor coverings in the poor houses.

There was a cobbler in the village. He made sandals, the soles of which were cut from the treads of old motor-car tyres. These tyres were bought by enterprising merchants in the city, and sold at considerable profit among the tribes. In spite of this, the sandals were inexpensive and I bought a pair for half-a-crown. They were excruciatingly uncomfortable, for they did not respond to the curvature of the foot. Several members of the party employed the cobbler to repair their shoes, but his efforts in this direction were even less successful. Peter was quite unable to get his feet into a pair of boots on which the cobbler had worked. Humphrey, however, managed to do so, and—unwilling to admit defeat—he hobbled about for several days before he broke them in.

As well as investigating local crafts, Humphrey studied the inter-relationships of various families in the village. But this was often difficult. He spent some time with pencil and paper after he was told: 'Ayisha is the niece of the wife of Mohammed ben Embark's uncle's son.'

Marriages in the valley were apparently arranged between the parents of the parties concerned; nevertheless, Berber women had a great deal more say in the choice of their husbands than did the Arab women. One of Humphrey's informants, Hussein ben Brahim, had a sad tale to tell:

Hussein had a great friend who was engaged, and the two of them went to stay with the girl's parents. The girl was mischievously inclined and during the course of their stay she told her younger sister that Hussein was in love with her. The sister apparently entered the room one day when they were eating, blushed a bright red, and fled in confusion. She went to her father, who knew nothing of the plot, and told him that Hussein wished to marry her. A few days after returning from the visit, the hero of this tale received a letter from the father, saying that he considered the match a very suitable one, and that he would shortly be calling on him to discuss the terms of the dowry. We did not hear the end of the story, but clearly the situation was difficult, for the father would consider a rebuff of his daughter as a personal affront.

During his inquiries Humphrey had to suffer the onslaughts of

Berber hospitality, and on one afternoon he returned to camp looking very sorry for himself. He was in no mood for conversation, but muttered that he had been obliged to eat no less than four lunches in succession.

Meanwhile Peter busied himself with the map, Colin and John went out on collecting expeditions, and I dealt with yet more patients, more sufferers from *imuslmen*, more 'brassières for Berbers'. There were, too, still many animals to be caught and preserved.

The stream outside our camp produced some interesting additions to my collections. It was crowded with animal life. Certainly its waters must have been nutritious, for they contained a very high proportion of decaying matter. The villagers had no qualms about using the stream for disposing of garbage, and one found in it the remains of dead goats, old clothes, and kitchen slops. There were many little scavengers, particularly beetles and mites, which fed on these remains, and they provided the food for frogs. The frogs in their turn were preyed upon by small snakes, which lay in the mud and which were cryptically coloured so that they were almost invisible. These snakes were popularly supposed to be poisonous, and we felt very courageous in collecting them. The technique was simple: we stirred up the mud with a stick until we disturbed a snake; one of us followed it until it settled, held down its head with the blade of a sheath-knife, and picked it up by its tail. Then he threw it into a butterfly net. After an hour's work we would have ten or fifteen snakes writhing about in the bottom of the net, which could be disconnected from its frame and pushed into a large bottle. A piece of cotton-wool soaked in anaesthetic was also placed in the bottle, and the whole thing was sealed until the snakes were dead. None of us was ever bitten.

An uninjured dead snake can be carried in the hand and made to wriggle in a very life-like fashion. We several times frightened Mohammed ben Hamed and Lhassan in this way.

The villagers could not understand why we wanted to collect animals, but eventually they decided that we were making medicines from them. Since explanations about 'The Advancement of Science' and the 'Good of Humanity' made little impression, we encouraged them in their misconceptions, and, at the same time, stimulated them to help us in finding animals.

We were pleased one day when two boys brought in a pair of ground squirrels which they had managed to catch in a home-made snare. But it was a blow to our pride, for these were the squirrels which had scorned our highly scientific mammal traps. Brahim spent a great deal of time and generated a lot of noise in building a cage, from which one immediately escaped. The other was not so fortunate, and we managed to bring him home to England. He fed happily on vegetable scraps and oatmeal biscuits, and although he seemed to be frightened he remained sleek and healthy. We called him 'Herbert', and he became the expedition pet.

Other animals were brought in, but they were mainly small ones: grasshoppers and scorpions. There was a regular collector of grass-hoppers, who would bring in ten or fifteen at a time in exchange for a cigarette. On one occasion Mohammed ben Hamed collected a large green lizard, which he had killed with a lucky sling-shot.

The men were very accurate with their slings, and they could hurl stones more than fifty yards. They spent a great deal of time trying to teach us the art, but the instruction was never successful. The sling was of heavy cord about four feet long, with a pouch in the middle to hold the stone. Both ends of the cord were held in the hand, the sling was whirled round the head several times, and then suddenly one of the ends was released. If this was done at the right moment the stone flew out at high speed in the required direction, and the loose end of the cord cracked like a whip. When we tried it, the stone either remained in the sling, or shot off in the wrong direction.

Lest they should think that Englishmen were incompetent at all manual skills I arranged a small deception. Pacing out a set distance from the walnut tree, I made a mark with a stick in the earth. From there I practised throwing my heavy sheath-knife, and afterwards when we had visitors I would stroll casually up to the mark and hurl the knife so that it stuck quivering in the tree trunk. The villagers were suitably impressed, but Mohammed ben Hamed said:

'It is not good for fighting. With your method you can only kill one man. We, by stabbing, can kill many.'

The Moroccan dagger, being curved, seems at first sight to be an inefficient weapon, but we realized that this was not so when we were shown how it was used. In attack, the handle of the dagger is clasped tightly in the fist, which is held palm downwards. The arm is crooked. A stabbing motion is imparted by straightening the arm away from the body, and the curve of the blade follows the trajectory of the fist. The movement resembles a backhand shot in tennis, except of course that the hand is differently placed. It is a much stronger movement than the conventional European stab.

The handles and sheaths of Berber daggers are often beautifully engraved, sometimes in silver and gold. In the markets of Marrakesh a good silver dagger costs about £15, and a gold one, of course, is even more expensive.

* * * *

Some of the rich men of the village, those, that is, who could afford to pay the Khalifa for the privilege, owned antique shotguns. They were no doubt useful for procuring game, but we never saw anyone out for a day's shooting. There seemed to be, in fact, a certain reticence in admitting ownership of firearms, although on one occasion Boghrib's *mohasni* came down to show us one of his cartridges. It contained a single heavy lead bullet which can have been useful only in shooting wild boar—or men. The hunt of wild boar was probably the most important single reason for the ownership of guns in the valley, and this might account for the reluctance of the villagers to admit that they possessed them. Boar-hunting was forbidden by French law, and there was also the suspicion that the flesh of these animals was eaten by the hunters—a practice abhorrent to orthodox Muslims.

I have already described the abortive expedition which John and I made in search of a boar. There was another occasion when a sow and her piglet were seen trotting across the hillside opposite Idirh. Lhassan came running to the camp shouting, '*Ilf, ilf,*' and waving his arms with excitement. We climbed up in pursuit of the beasts, and discovered that the whole village had turned out for the hunt. The villagers spent a great part of the day running aimlessly about the mountain sides. But although they found tracks of the animals, they did not see them, and in the evening returned home despondently.

* * * *

During our stay I tried to draw up a dictionary of unusual Berber words. It was not a very good one, because I found it difficult to transscribe into English letters many of the strange sounds which make up the language. It was difficult enough to pronounce them, and in fact my efforts gave a great deal of amusement to the villagers. People would come to the camp specifically to hear me pronounce the Berber for 'spoon'. It can inadequately be written as *taranjaout*. The difficulty to the European lies in the first *r*, which is a strange rolling guttural similar to the Scottish *r*, but pronounced further back in the throat.

The dictionary gave us clues to the extent of local knowledge of natural history. The larger animals all had individual names: *Ilf* (wild boar), *oudad* (mouflons), or *tazlemoumouit* (lizard). The same was true of some of the smaller ones, such as *tabakha* (spider), *izan* (fly), and *abiba* (daddy-long-legs). Many of them, however, did not have such names, and there was a portmanteau word for unspecific creepy-crawlies—*lbkhoushen*. There was no apparent knowledge of astronomy; *aiour, tafoukt,* and *itren,* were the moon, sun, and stars respectively. But there were no names, it seemed, for individual stars or constellations. Judging from the normal method of forming plurals in Berber, the singular of 'stars' should be *atre* if the plural is *itren*. *Atre* bears a strong resemblance to the Latin 'astra'. Could it be that this is another word taken from the Romans?

There were certain peculiarities in anatomical description. There was no distinction, for instance, between vein and artery—they were both called *azrourh*; but the vocabulary did note the difference between cartilage and bone. Each of the fingers had a different name, but this was not so of the toes. The molar teeth are known as *isrien*—a word which literally means 'millstones'.

* * * *

We had spent altogether seven weeks in Idirh when the time came for us to leave. We were reluctant to go; there was so much more to be done, so much more to learn about the people of the valley. But we had plans to visit the south before returning to England, and the end of our vacation was drawing near.

Before our departure we tried to sum up our impressions of the valley. Humphrey's concern was to describe the social organization of the Glaoua tribe. In travel pamphlets, with photographs of magnificent horsemen against unclouded skies, the Berbers of Morocco have been called 'liberty-loving democrats'. This is true, but more particularly of tribes other than the Glaoua. Among the people in the region round Telouet the rule of el-Glaoui had been superimposed upon the 'democratic' Berber society. The rule was a harsh one. It could be described as feudal, though this too would be an over-simplification.

The villagers were certainly in subjection. The Pasha was apparently all-powerful; he could command them to provide mules, or to work in his fields; he could command them to act as his soldiers in Marrakesh; they were obliged from time to time to serve as sentries at the *kasbah* of Telouet. The Pasha's power was absolute, but at the same time it was remote, and demands of this sort—although arbitrary—were occasional. Furthermore, within the villages the tribesmen were free to exercise democratic control over their own affairs. They could plant what crops they wished, they could arrange their life to suit themselves. It was even possible for them to take the law into their own hands, and, as in the case of the man who was caught stealing figs, to exact their own punishment. This freedom was probably greater at the time of our visit that it had been in the past. I have already mentioned that the power of the Pasha was waning, and that the people were in a state of vacillation between their traditional loyalty to his person and their sympathy with the Nationalists.

They could protest quite vigorously against injustice, and we were told that in one of the villages the Pasha's tax-collectors had been stoned by an angry crowd. It is surprising that no punishment was exacted for this defiance of authority.

It is not possible conveniently to sum up the social system of the Glaoua by describing it as democratic, or oligarchic, or feudal. Terms of this sort were designed to describe Western societies, and it is not legitimate to employ them elsewhere. We can only say that the system of government among the Glaoua had qualities of all three.

In spite of this there were many superficial resemblances between life in the valley and life as it must have been in medieval Europe; the hierarchy of Khalifa-Sheikh-Mokkodem tribesmen; the very complete system of mutual responsibility and hospitality; the primitive medical remedies and agricultural techniques; the pre-French strife between petty war lords—all these added up to a picture of medieval European life.

Humphrey was interested in social systems, but he and I also wanted to know whether we had really come to understand the individual people in the valley. It was a subject about which we were equally unsure. Sentimentally we liked to imagine that these men were our friends, that they valued our company not merely because we had things to give them. But it was difficult to be sure. Hospitality and kindness to visitors were so much a part of the Moroccan way of life that perhaps the people would have welcomed anyone as they welcomed us. We would happily imagine that we understood these people, then suddenly they would behave in a manner which seemed unreasonable or unkind, and we would be forced to realize how much our differences meant, how senseless it was to expect a genuine friendship across the barriers of race and creed.

Perhaps Humphrey and I were too interested in motives. Peter and John tended much more to accept the Berbers at face value, and possibly they were right. There are many pitfalls for one who attempts to *explain* human behaviour.

Whatever their motives, the people of the valley begged us to postpone our departure.

'You must wait,' they said, 'so that we can give you a feast.'

The Sheikh went even further.

'You must stay with us, M'soor Chef. You must stay with us and treat our illnesses. We will give you a house and wife. I have a girl in mind for you. She is young and very beautiful. She will work hard for you, and she will satisfy all your desires.'

He grinned salaciously, and went on to sketch out in embarrassing detail her numerous attractions. I was almost tempted to ask him for her on approval, and it was an appealing idea to stay in this isolated village, to live in reasonable comfort with one or two wives to do the hard work, to make a modest living treating the inhabitants for their ailments, and to forget the need for gaining a degree and finding a job. A man could be peaceful and happy in the Ait Rbaa, but how long, I wondered, would it last? How soon would one crave for the comforts of the Western way of life, and how soon would Western civilization itself come to the valley, improving the material well-being of its people, but not perhaps making them happier or more content.

We loaded our belongings on to the mule-train, and started out for the last time along the path to Telouet. We passed the terraced fields, we climbed the black cinder-covered slopes, we left behind Idirh and Titullah and Anammer. Later I stood at the summit of the pass, and looked back over the green ribbon of the Ait Rbaa. Even after so short a time the flat-roofed villages seemed a great distance away. Soon they would fade into the dim realms of memory. We would return to England, to an existence so different that we would be unable to remember the details of our life in the valley. A vague picture might remain, but we would perhaps fail to recollect the vision of evening shadows slanting across the valley, or the sound of shepherds singing on the mountain sides. Memories are strengthened by chance impressions—by sights and sounds which remind one of other such sights and sounds—by words and phrases which remind one of other words and phrases. But the worlds of the present and the past would be so remote from one another. It was difficult to imagine that our recollections could be sustained.

The men of Idirh carried our equipment to Telouet, and I bade them a sentimental farewell in the courtyard of the Kasbah.

'*Bislammah*, M'soor Chef,' they said. '*Bislammah*.'

'*Bislammah*. God be with you.'

'You will come back, *insha'allah*?'

'*Insha'allah*, if God wills.'

Some of them looked really sad—one even had tears in his eyes when he clasped my hand. Did the laws of Berber hospitality stretch so far? Or had we perhaps built a genuine bridge across the gulf that separated us? I remembered our first vision of the Arab on the donkey. The gulf, it seemed, was not as wide as we had thought then.

CHAPTER TEN

The Encroaching Desert

Homme, si, le coeur plein de joie ou d'amertume,
Tu passais vers midi dans les champs radieux,
Fuis! la nature est vide et le soleil consume:
Rien n'est vivant ici, rien n'est triste ou joyeux.

LECONTE DE LISLE

BETWEEN 9 and 11 September, Telouet suffered what must have been the greatest invasion of the English in its long history.

Peter stayed in Idirh to continue with his map, but the rest of us came to the *kasbah*, and we were joined, not only by Thesiger, but also by the Gellners, who had driven to Telouet from Zaouia Ahansal.

The Khalifa was away, but his second-in-command entertained us royally—there was more mint-tea in silver teapots, and there was a succession of extravagant concoctions of mutton. He promised to make arrangements for the several journeys that we planned. John and Thesiger intended to walk south-west from Telouet along the Atlas, and to climb Djebel Toubkal, the highest mountain in North Africa. Humphrey was to join the Gellners on a drive through the oases of the River Draa. Colin and I decided to take the truck and drive south, to collect animals in the desert.

On the tenth John and Thesiger left in one of the Pasha's trucks for a nearby village, whence they would begin their journey on foot. Colin and I remained in Telouet until the following day. Omar, a *mohasni*, was appointed as our bodyguard for the journey south. He was a short, thickset, dissipated-looking man, with the drooping eyes of the hashish addict. Dressed as he was in a jet-black *djellaba*, he had an extremely villainous appearance.

'Tartarin' rumbled out of Telouet on the evening of the eleventh, Colin and I in the cab and Omar dozing in the back. We drove slowly to the main road, and turned left in the direction of Ouazazate.

On the way up a steep hill 'Tartarin' stalled. We could not push the truck forward; the only way to get it started was to reverse down the hill—a hazardous proceeding when the night was dark and the road curved round the edge of a steep precipice. Very carefully we released the brake and rolled backwards. When we had reached a good speed, Colin let in the clutch, and with a tremendous jolt the truck came suddenly to a halt. Then from behind us we heard a shout of dismay. Omar, sleeping in the back, had been thrown out on the road—with a great deal of luggage on top of him. This did not improve his temper. We repacked the truck, put Omar in the front, and tried again. Eventually we managed to start the engine.

As we bowled along the dark curling roadway, I could see the faces of Colin and the *mohasni*, illuminated by the light from the dashboard. Colin had a look of fierce concentration as he steered the truck round hairpin bends and past sleeping villages. Omar sat staring into space, with the *kief* pipe gripped between his teeth. From time to time he grunted.

When, about a quarter of an hour later, we came to the halting place of Irherm n'Ougdal, I tried to improve Omar's state of mind—which seemed to be one of venomous disapproval. I offered to buy him a Pepsi-Cola, an offer which he condescended to accept. So we parked the truck, and made our way into the bar of the inn. It was a long low room, full of smoke, and crowded with Moroccan workmen from the nearby *téléférique*. One of them, apparently, was an acquaintance of the *mohasni*, for he came up behind him, and laid a hand heavily upon his shoulder.

Omar was taken by surprise, but I have never seen a man move so quickly. In a second the *mohasni* had his assailant pinned against the wall, with the point of a dagger hovering a quarter of an inch from his throat. There was sensation in the *cantine*, people crowded round, and the *patron* came out from behind the bar, protesting that this was not the sort of behaviour to be expected in *his* establishment.

Omar's victim, feeling no doubt that discretion was the better part of valour, apologized profusely—and was eventually released. I hurried the *mohasni* out of the inn, and into the truck. He never got his Pepsi-Cola.

*   *   *   *

We arrived in the garrison town of Ouazazate at about 10 p.m., found a plantation of trees at the edge of the settlement, and put down our beds. Omar, for the first time, became concerned about our welfare.

'You must not sleep here,' he said. 'You will be robbed.'

'But we have you to protect us.'

'Alone, I would not be sufficient—there are many evil men here.'

But by now we knew the Moroccan's mistrust of anyone who is not born in his own village—a mistrust often taken to ridiculous lengths. There is a proverb, all-embracing in its condemnation of strangers:

'Everyone from afar is a great deceiver.'

So we did not heed the *mohasni's* protests, and continued with our preparations for bed. Eventually, with very ill grace, he departed, muttering ominously under his breath. We wondered if he had decided to forsake us completely, leaving us to face the consequences of our own 'foolishness'. But we misjudged him; half an hour later he returned with two companions, and they all settled down to sleep a short distance away from us. I never discovered where or how he managed to obtain those extra guards.

The following morning we had a look at the town. The place was full of soldiers, for Ouazazate is an important military centre in the Sahara, and was the base from which French troops subdued many of the desert tribes. The town has two cafés, a military hospital, and several barracks. It reminded me, for some reason, of a settlement in the early days of the American West.

About a mile to the east of the town there is the fantastic mud *kasbah* of Taourirt, a fortified town whose ramparts rise sixty or seventy feet above the surrounding desert, whose square towers, pierced by innumerable windows and surmounted by white battlements, house many hundreds of people. Taourirt was the home of one of el-Glaoui's most important Khalifas, who superintended the affairs of the Ait Ouaouzguit—a confederation of tribes which stretched from Ouazazate to the arid mountains of the Djebel Siroua.

Situated on the direct route from Telouet to the Draa, the palmery of Ouazazate has always been of strategic importance, and in order to protect the trade route the Almohad Sultans built there a *kasbah* which housed their garrisons. This *kasbah*, known as Irherm n'Ougellid— 'The Fortress of the King'—remained for several centuries, and must have been visited by Sultan Ahmed el Mansour during his march to Timbuctoo in quest of Songhai gold. Some fragments of it can be seen near the French Military Post. The present *kasbah* of Taourirt is a more recent construction.

K

We breakfasted at one of the little tables outside the Café de la Légion, and watched the town coming slowly to morning life. A squad of soldiers marched smartly down the dusty road; opposite, a little shop was opening its shutters. It sold everything from wines to watches, and the proprietor was busily polishing a number of fat melons which he intended to display in his window. Military lorries trundled by, then a long Buick with a turbaned dignitary lounging in the back.

We discussed plans, and decided to base ourselves at the oasis at Agdz, which lay about forty-five miles to the south-east in the valley of the River Draa. We hoped that 'Tartarin' would behave well, for we would be travelling on a road which carried little traffic and which crossed regions of waterless desert.

We filled our jerry-cans, some with water, some with petrol, and drove out of the palm-groves of Ouazazate.

The road led into a country of low hills, whose bare rocks fiercely reflected the heat of the sun. Soon we reached a piece of high ground, and saw, rolling away in the distance, miles and miles of monotonous red-brown desert. 'Tartarin' rumbled through the dry solitude, and inside the cab the temperature became suffocating.

It is difficult to describe a desert except in negatives. It lacks vegetation, animals, and human beings. It lacks, at any rate during the day, variations in colour. The only positive thing is the heat. The desert is a hard, impersonal, unfriendly void. Yet there is something about its very emptiness which is fascinating. There is little detail to distract the eye, little sound to engage the ear, no smell. In the absence of sensory impressions the mind is free from the forces that normally bind it to the body. It is free to take a larger view, to relate the part to the whole. In the desert, I felt, self-importance was lost; man saw himself as a mere cog in the vast machine of nature. Yet he was better able to apprehend the purpose of this machine, and in recognizing his own insignificance he realized more clearly the significance of the whole. It became clear to me why the mystics had gone to the desert for their meditations. Their task of subduing the passions and desires of the body, of suppressing the individuality of the mind, would be easier here. In the desert man is alone with himself. . . .

This was all very well, but in practice we were alone in the desert with 'Tartarin', and the truck was beginning to cough and splutter like an aged smoker. But it did not stop, not at any rate until we came to a narrow river which flowed sluggishly between ranks of palm trees. Here we drew to a halt, filled the radiator and made a quick dash to the river to collect frogs. Then we were off again across a concrete causeway, and we plunged once more into a region of arid desolation. Now the scenery was more interesting, for the hills were higher and some of them had been eroded by the wind and sand into fantastic towers and pinnacles. But it was still a lonely place, and the harshness of it awed me a little.

At one point we stopped for a drink, and Colin climbed a small hill to take a photograph. Sitting in the cab in the heat and the silence, I watched the rocks on the opposite side of the road shimmering in hot currents of air. Omar, who had been sitting in the back, solidly smoking his *kief*, came round to join me. We chatted for a while in pidgin Arabic, and then he noticed my sheath-knife.

'That is a good knife,' he said. 'May I look at it?'

I gave it to him, and he examined it carefully, stroking the blade appreciatively with his thumb. Then he gripped the handle, pointed the knife towards me, and gazed at me for a long time through half-closed eyes. Then suddenly the knife flashed in the sun, and he lunged straight towards me. I parried the blow, and in my fright fell back over the gear lever. Omar laughed heartily—in a nasty sort of way—and retired to the back of the truck.

Half an hour later we began to climb a range of black rock, and passing over it descended into a wide valley, where there was a green oasis. This was Ait Saoun, which harbours an isolated tribe of pure Berbers—pure, that is, in race, although possibly also in morals; in the region of the oasis there are many bushes of which the fruit, carried as an amulet, enjoys a widespread reputation for preserving chastity. The people of Ait Saoun are shepherds, and spend a great part of the year wandering in the mountains, sleeping in little portable huts which are constructed of oleander wood and roofed with hemp matting. They come down to the oasis only in the winter.

Ait Saoun is a pleasant place after the barren desert. It has fruit trees and gardens and springs of fresh water welling up among the palms. We were tempted to linger there, but the French Post at Agdz had been warned that we would arrive that evening, and if we did not appear, parties would be sent out to search for us. Such precautions were irritating but necessary. It has happened that travellers on the road have broken down, and died of thirst before help reached them.

We took more water than the average traveller, but then 'Tartarin' was less dependable than the average car.

We left the oasis and drove out across the flat gravel plain. A few miles beyond Ait Saoun the road began to climb a range of black basalt mountains. It rose in a series of tortuous loops to cross them on the pass of Tizin'Tinifift. Here, at a height of 5,000 feet, we could look back to the green patch of Ait Saoun, and forward across the endless series of arid mountain tops. Far over to the left was the great bleak outcrop of the Djebel Sahro.

A mile beyond the pass we saw for the first time the vast black canyons of the River Ourika, which meandered thousands of feet below us. We could not see the river itself, for the water moved below the surface of the ground, but its course was marked by a ribbon of low bushes, and a camel-track followed the dry river-bed. At one point a small party of men were plodding wearily along it, with a single camel.

The road wound vertiginously down the steep sides of the canyon, and as we descended we came to an area where the rocks changed in colour from brown to green. Turning a corner, we suddenly saw—spread out far below us—the wide palm-covered valley of the Draa. There were thousands and thousands of palm trees receding into the distant haze, and beyond them red mountains rolling back like waves on the seashore. We coasted down to the valley, past a ruined mud fortress, and reached the town of Agdz as the sun set behind the jagged peaks.

Agdz lies at a point where a tributary of the Draa joins the main stream. Between the two rivers a sharp ridge of rock juts out into the sandy plain. On the opposite bank there is another smaller ridge, on the summit of which there is a French fortress.

The Commandant, when we visited him, very kindly offered us guest rooms in the fort. We accepted his offer gladly, but did not expect, in this isolated place, a high standard of comfort. We were in for a surprise. A French soldier showed us to our rooms. Each of them was luxuriously appointed; there were thick carpets, modern paintings on the walls, very comfortable double beds, electric lights—and private bathrooms! It seemed that the French, when they were building their outposts in the desert, were not to be deterred by difficult conditions. The fort bore a strong resemblance to the Ritz.

Now that we were so well established we decided that our *mohasni* could be dispensed with, and asked the Commandant to dismiss him for us.

Omar must have been a naturally discontented man. It was clear that he did not enjoy being with us, but he was even more unhappy when we told him to go. The Khalifa, he said, would have him thrashed when he discovered that we were displeased with his services; we hastened to reassure him, untruthfully, that he had been invaluable. But he still looked unhappy.

We spent the next day collecting animals among the palms. We dug for earthworms in the irrigation ditches which meandered through the oasis; we chased butterflies across the alfalfa fields; we captured the fat beetles that crouched under stones by the river. In the afternoon we went a small distance along the road to chase bright red fat-tailed lizards; but it was not a productive hunt. After several hours we had only caught one small, rather anaemic-looking specimen. The ones that got away were all of enormous size and gaudy colour. We continued collecting until late in the evening, and as the sun set we saw a remarkable sight. Bats, which had been sleeping in the palm trees and the houses and in the surrounding rocks, came out to feed. They came out all at once, and congregated together in a huge flock. There must have been thousands of them, and they flew squeaking and chattering in a huge cloud that swept by us, to disappear into the distance.

During the following days we made excursions into the surrounding desert. As time went by we learnt to recognize places where animals would be most common, but nevertheless collecting was a tiring business. We would turn over a hundred stones before finding one that sheltered some form of life. There was an element of excitement, for one never knew what would appear under the next stone. It might be a lizard or a small snake, a scorpion or a long poisonous centipede. Sometimes there were beetles, invariably black ones, and sometimes solifugids—spider-like animals with enormous biting jaws.

The desert in the south of Morocco has not always been such. Five thousand years ago Morocco was a fertile land. At that time it was more humid than it is today, and Latin and Greek authors record the occurrence of lions, elephants and hippopotami. Pliny states that crocodiles once swam in the River Draa. Since then the climate has become progressively drier. The vegetation south of the Atlas was over-grazed by sheep and goats, and destroyed at a rate greater than it could replace itself. The sun baked away the fertile soil, and the desert crept northwards. Even in recent times the Draa valley has been drying up, and during our travels in the south we saw many villages and castles that had been abandoned because there was no longer sufficient water to support human life. Arab historians called the Draa 'The Valley of Olives', but these trees have now almost completely disappeared, and the few which remain are poor and unproductive. In spite of its decreasing fertility, the Draa still supports more than a million date-palms, many plantations of fruit trees and fields of barley and maize. Among the palms there are oleanders and tamarisks. In the latter are found galls, caused by a fly which pierces the leaves in order to lay its eggs. The inhabitants call these galls *takaout*, and collect them in autumn when they become mature. The *takaout* contains more than 50 per cent of tanning substances, and the tribesmen use them in the preparation of leather. The famous 'Morocco' leather is produced in this manner.

There are three races of men inhabiting the Draa valley: the Arabs, the Berbers—some of whom belong to the Ait Atta and are desert 'brothers' of the tribes encountered by Colin—and the Haratin. The Haratin are dark men, whose origins have been much disputed. They are generally considered to be of mixed blood, half Berber and half Negro. It is certain that many Negroes came to inhabit the Draa valley, for they were brought from the Sudan as slaves by conquering Berber chieftains. There are also a small number of Jews, who at one time were widespread in the valley. But they have lost their influence, and now there are only three small *mellahs*.

*   *   *   *

On one of our collecting expeditions Colin and I took the road which led in the direction of the cobalt mines at Bou Azzer. A few miles from Agdz we parked the truck, and set off to climb one of the nearby mountain ridges. The sun blazed out of a clear sky, and the rocks blazed back. A few grasshoppers staggered about on the burning slopes, and we staggered after them. We reached the top of the ridge to find a valley, in the bottom of which was a single bedraggled bush, and beyond it another identical ridge. We climbed down—and up again. From the second ridge the view was identical. There was a certain monotony about the scenery which discouraged further exploration, so we went down into one of the valleys and sat under 'the bush'.

I was perspiring in its shade, looking up at the ridge we had just crossed, when a human head and shoulders appeared above it. This was very surprising; we were nowhere near a mule-track, nor was there any vegetation for grazing sheep. I came out from under my bush to get a better view, but the figure on the ridge saw me and threw himself down the other side, so that he disappeared from sight. I called Colin, and we returned to the truck to make sure that nothing had been stolen. Nothing had; and we saw no more of our mysterious watcher. But I remembered, or thought I remembered, one thing about him: he seemed to be in uniform. Could it be that the Commandant had sent one of his men to keep an eye on us? Was he perhaps worried about our safety, or even about our intentions?

On the same day, at another place, we were wandering among the rocks when suddenly we disturbed a small animal, which fled from us in a series of bounds, leaping from rock to rock, and finally disappear-into a crevice. Colin put his hand into the crack, and brought out a little grey-brown creature that looked at us fearfully from large circular eyes. It was about nine inches long and a very odd shape in-deed, with enormous back legs, like a kangaroo, and a long thin flexible snout which made him resemble, from the front, a miniature elephant. And indeed this resemblance gives rise to the name of the group to which he belonged—the elephant shrews.

We put him into a box, and he snuffled about squeaking in a rather pathetic way. We brought him home to the fort and fed him on bread and milk—a difficult business, because he was reluctant to eat. We called him 'Willis', and he lived for a while in a biscuit tin. He had an appealing habit, when one opened his tin, of pressing his nose on the ground so that the snout curled upwards, and looking up trustingly. Then one day on the way home somebody left his tin in the sun, and he died of heat-stroke. I was very annoyed and distressed about this, for we had become more attached to Willis than to any of our other animals.

* * * *

Agdz, like many other places in Morocco, was at its best in the evening. Then the colours were heightened, the light was soft, people came out of their houses and moved about in the shade of the palms. The day's work was done; there was an atmosphere of relaxation and friendliness. As the night fell, lights sprang up all over the valley. Strolling past the tall mud *kasbahs* we caught glimpses of chambers bright with the unsteady light of flaming torches that were set in their walls. The sound of voices or of music drifted across on the night air, and behind, on the unfriendly hills, came the cries of jackals.

*   *   *   *

Colin and I spent four days in Agdz before returning to Ouazazate, where we had arranged to meet Humphrey and Peter. At the Café de la Légion we gathered together, and exchanged accounts of our journeys.

Humphrey had driven with the Gellners along the same road to Agdz, but they had continued south by the Draa to the last major oasis at Zagora, where there are ruined cities believed by some to be the remains of Roman trading posts. A few miles to the south-east of Zagora they visited the *zaouia* of Tamgrout. In this little village they found a company of potters, who got their clay from the banks of a nearby stream. They used massive wooden wheels about two feet in diameter and weighing forty pounds, which they turned with their feet. The pots were baked, about three hundred at a time in large wood-burning ovens, and afterwards were glazed in yellow and green. For their glazes the potters employed native antimony and copper. For festive occasions they produced curious spinning-tops known as *merraias*, which were sold in all the markets of the Draa. Humphrey brought back samples not only of their pots, but also of their clay and glazes.

From Tamgrout Humphrey and the Gellners returned northwards, and then branched east into the wastes of the Djebel Sahro. Here, at Tazzarine, they were entertained by the only French official in the area; they were his first visitors for many months. Then they returned to Ouazazate.

Peter had remained in Idirh while he completed the map. He came down from Telouet on the bus.

Peter wanted to see something of the south, so we decided that he and I should drive down the River Zguid, a stream which ran to the west of the Draa and parallel to it. Humphrey, Colin and M'Barek would walk from Tamdaght back to Telouet—a distance of about thirty miles.

Tamdaght lay some way to the north of Ouazazate, and was joined to the main road by a rutted track. The truck bounced along it, across low desert hills, and past the imposing towers of the village of Ait ben

Haddou. Rounding a final corner, we came to the elegant *kasbah* of
Tamdaght, home of one of el-Glaoui's Khalifas. Tamdaght, in its way,
is even more impressive than Telouet, its walls are completely white,
its massive pointed gates are painted blue.

We parked the truck outside and were greeted by the Khalifa, who
led us through courtyards with tiled and decorated doorways, into a
long low room which had silk cushions scattered across its carpets. The
Khalifa told us that we were the first Englishmen to visit the *kasbah*,
and over luncheon he gave us an account of its history.

The fortress, he said, used to belong to the Ait Ouasguita tribe, but
their last Sheikh rebelled against the authority of the Glaoua. He
blocked the caravan route to Ouazazate and robbed any who attempted
to pass by. El-Glaoui came out against him with a great force of men,
and with a cannon, but he bombarded the fortress in vain, and the
Sheikh was beaten only because of the treason of one of his followers.
He was coming out of the *kasbah* at the head of his forces when someone shut the gate behind him. He was left to face the enemy alone. He
tried to run away but was killed, and the fortress was taken.

The luncheon was a good one. It started with loaves of barley bread,
fresh butter and honey, and was followed by a partridge *kus kus*. There
was also, of course, mint-tea.

Afterwards Colin, Humphrey and M'Barek remained at Tamdaght.
They spent the night there before starting their walk to Telouet. Peter
and I returned to Ouazazate.

*   *   *   *

The following morning we charged 'Tartarin' with petrol and
drove off towards the French Post of Tazenakht, which was our first
stopping place on the road to Foum Zguid.

The scenery was similar to that on the way to Agdz, and the succession of abandoned mud villages told the same sad story of drying
water sources and encroaching desert. But here the situation was more
serious. There was hardly an inhabited village between Ouazazate and
Tazenakht. Men had striven for the control of southern Morocco,
lives had been lost in its assault and defence, but the ultimate victor was
the desert, making a mockery of human endeavour. Yet, as I have said,
the desert itself was due largely to the activities of man, to the excessive
grazing of his flocks. As elsewhere in Morocco, human communities
had sown the seeds of their own destruction.

Tazenakht lies on a flat sandy plain about forty miles south of Ouazazate. There is a French fort, a *cantine*, and a few scattered houses, all constructed of red mud bricks. We arrived there in the late afternoon, and waited in the forecourt of the fort. A *mohasni* led us to the Commandant, who very kindly offered us rooms.

While we were unpacking some of our belongings from the truck, we were surprised to see clouds gathering in the west. A few minutes later a wind sprang up, and drops of rain began to fall. The wind increased in force—then suddenly the sand came. Choking yellow dust stung our faces, and we could no longer see from one side of the courtyard to the other. The grit blew into our clothes, into our eyes, and we breathed it into our lungs. We fled for cover, and for a full twenty minutes the sand-storm raged about the fort. Looking out from the windows we thought it looked like a blizzard; but the 'snow' was yellow. Then it ended as suddenly as it had begun, and we came out to find everything coated with sand.

I strolled outside the fort. The sun was setting in the west, where there was a patch of bright blue sky. To the east was the sand-storm that had just passed—an enormous bank of dust sloping upwards from the ground, bright red in the setting sun. Immediately above us was grey cloud, from which a little rain was still falling, and against the red sand billows there was a double rainbow. It was the most beautiful sunset I have seen.

*   *   *   *

The drive from Tazenakht to Foum Zguid took us across another sandy plain beside more deserted villages. There was, however, one oasis which was still inhabited, and here there was a series of tree-trunks laid across the road. We wondered what was the purpose of this road-block, and waited by it uncertainly. No one came. Then we sounded the horn, and two little figures carrying rifles hurried towards us. We were relieved to discover that they were soldiers of the French Army.

'Are you the English?' they asked.

'Yes. Why is there a road-block?'

'We're checking all the traffic. There's been trouble in the manganese mines. Several people have been killed. We want to make sure that it doesn't spread. We'll telephone through to Foum Zguid that you're on the way.'

For the rest of the journey we drove alongside the bed of the River Zguid, which cut through a range of mountains before debouching into the flat desert. The word *Foum* means a gap in a mountain range, and Foum Zguid lies at the point where the river issues out into the flat *hammada*, or gravel plain, of the Sahara. On each side of the gap there is a castle—to the west a Moroccan *kasbah*, to the east a French fort. Between them, stretching out a short distance into the plain, are the palms of the oasis.

At the fort we met Capitaine Tallyrand, and again we were given luxurious rooms with private baths and showers. Capitaine Tallyrand told us that the fortress even had a swimming pool. He was apologetic that it was empty for cleaning. Our rooms opened out on the flat roof of the fort, and in the evening we stood on the battlements looking out over the oasis. Beyond the palms, for many miles, the *hammada* stretched flat and featureless, until in the far distance it was interrupted by a low range of hills.

Beyond them no doubt it stretched on and on for thousands of miles, relieved perhaps in places by ranks of sand-dunes. But all was desert, all was dry and bare and hostile. It did not come to an end in the south until it reached the banks of the Niger, nor in the west until the Rio de Oro, where the desert meets the shores of the Atlantic Ocean. This was the coast which, thousands of years ago, had supplied Phoenician traders with gold, which had been visited by the ships of Hanno on his voyage to Central Africa, and perhaps also—between 610 and 595 B.C.—by the officers of the Egyptian Pharaoh Neco, who circumnavigated Africa from the Red Sea to Gibraltar.

Capitaine and Madame Tallyrand entertained us to dinner. The dining-room was cool and dark, and the table was lit by candles. Silver shone on its polished surface, and the meal was served by a white-coated attendant. We had soup, and an exquisite steak, washed down with good wine. It was difficult to believe that we were in a place where supplies came but once a month.

Capitaine Tallyrand was devoted to his job. Single-handed he administered an area the size of Yorkshire; there was not another European for forty miles in any direction. He talked enthusiastically of irrigation schemes to improve the fertility of the valley, of methods encouraging production of pottery and carpets, of the formation of co-operatives to buy modern agricultural implements. His influence in the Zguid was obviously not due to force; the only soldiers in the fort were half a dozen *Goums*. He was accepted by the tribes because they respected him, and because he respected them. It was sad to think that dedicated men of this type—and there were many of them in the Service des Affaires Indigenes—should be betrayed in their work by the vacillations of the Government which they served. Capitaine Tallyrand was too loyal a Frenchman to admit this, and perhaps the strife in Morocco had not yet affected his region. But the time would no doubt come when racial hatred would drive him and his kind from their posts. The loss would be to the people whom they administered.

That meal with the Tallyrands was the best we had eaten on the whole journey. It is strange that it should have been at our remotest point from home.

*   *   *   *

Peter and I spent peaceful days at Foum Zguid, and wandered on the dry slopes of the range collecting animals, beetles, scorpions, and the remarkable snails which wait, sealed in their shells, until the rain comes so that they can feed and breed. Sometimes they wait for many years. Their endurance is famous among zoologists, and there is a story that several of these snails were collected in the Sahara and taken back to the British Museum in London. There they were displayed in a case, and years after they had been collected they were put in water to be washed. The snails came out, and crawled about searching for food!

The slopes above Foum Zguid were crossed by thick stone walls, which ran in straight lines across them. No one could tell us when they had been built, or what purpose they had served. They did not seem to be defending any particular point; they cannot have been to enclose flocks, and they were certainly not boundaries of agricultural land. Even in the days when Morocco was more fertile, it is difficult to imagine that those particular slopes were cultivable, for they were steep and stony.

About a mile to the north of the fort there were the ruins of a mud *kasbah*, now the haunt only of scorpions and lizards. Behind it was a Muslim graveyard, a flat, open area, which looked very much like the rest of the desert but for the rough unlettered stones which stood at the head and the foot of each grave. There were no clues to the identity of the men who lay buried there. They were anonymous in their death and, after all, what use are names to the dead? The voice of cynicism whispered: '*Si monumentum requiris, circumspice.* Men have worked here; there is a desert.'

* * * *

We returned once more to Tazenakht, and stayed overnight in the fort. The Commandant showed us a couple of gazelles which his men had caught on the nearby plains. They were small creatures about three feet high, with thin spindly legs, and they seemed incredibly fragile. But we learnt that this was a false impression when we tried to hold one down so that we could photograph it. The gazelles roamed the plains in declining herds, and until the coming of the French their major enemy was man, for the local inhabitants used to hunt them on horseback. It was no easy matter, for the animals have a tremendous turn of speed. The Commandant told us that he had followed some in his car; they were travelling at well over forty miles an hour.

Also at Tazenakht we saw a Museum of Moroccan Arts and Crafts, where women were weaving carpets on the primitive vertical Moroccan looms. There were gay designs in black and white and red, but we could not afford to buy even the smallest carpet. The cheapest was about £7.

It was strange that the French should have set up this exhibit in a place like Tazenakht, which cannot have had a great number of visitors over the year; strange, and yet characteristic of their desire to impress the tourist with the good influences of France on Morocco. I felt this in all our contacts with the French authorities—that they were trying desperately hard to give one a good impression. Yet it seemed to me they went about it in the wrong way, by trying to guide the visitor to the places that they wished him to see, by showing him a façade of civilized advancement. How much more impressive it was to talk to an enthusiast like Capitaine Tallyrand than to see a rather dreary museum of arts and crafts! The French, I felt, had let their colonial inferiority complex get the better of their good judgement. They have indeed done tremendous things in Morocco, and how much more forcefully would they be brought home to the traveller if he were left to discover them for himself.

The following day we drove back through Ouazazate towards Telouet. At Ihrerm n'Ougdal we stopped for a drink at the *cantine—*

the scene of Omar's fracas. The proprietor was good enough to over-look our previous misdemeanours and provided us with very welcome refreshments. Sitting at one of the ugly marble-topped tables we got into conversation with a young French Army officer. He was in com-mand, he said, of a small military post which guarded the *téléférique*, and he invited us to spend the night there. We drove past the great metal shed where lorries from the manganese mines loaded the ore on to the little aerial trolleys. Behind the shed there were three Nissen huts, surrounded by a barbed wire fence. A soldier with a tommy gun ran to open the gate, and we drove in. One of the huts served as a combined armoury and mess-room, and it was here that we shared supper with the platoon. I talked to one of the junior N.C.O.s.

'Certainly it's lonely here,' he said. 'We eat and sleep in the compound, and we rarely go out, except to patrol the *téléférique*. There have been terrorists sabotaging it, and we've lost a number of our companions in fights with them. But the cable is very long, and it's almost impossible to guard it efficiently. We're better armed than the saboteurs, but sometimes they lie in ambush for us. It's a strain.'

In the evening an Arab N.C.O. suggested that we should all go out for a stroll. As we were setting off he asked us, 'Have you got your pistols with you?'

'No, we don't carry them.'

'That is very foolish. These Berbers here are villains. They will rob you and cut your throat if you are not armed.'

It was the old story, and I did not bother to point out that we had been living for two months with 'the villains'. It was noticeable that all the native troops in the platoon were Arabs. This is the way things are organized by the French. In the Berber regions they use Arab soldiers, and in the Arab regions, Berbers—taking advantage of the mistrust that exists between the two races. The Nationalists accuse the French of a policy of 'divide and conquer'. Possibly the accusation is justified, but it is an obvious military precaution. It would be un-satisfactory if the soldiers had emotional ties with the people of the region. It would be too easy for terrorists to bring pressure to bear upon them.

It was sad, though, that these men should have to live in their barbed wire enclosures with no understanding whatsoever of the people out-side it, with no feeling for them except that they were villains. Their ignorance bred fear, and their fear gave rise to hostility; there was no hope of understanding. It was sad, but inevitable.

*   *   *   *

Humphrey, Colin and M'Barek were waiting for us at the *kasbah* of Telouet. They had walked north from Tamdaght along the green valley of the River Ounila, a valley which ran through deep gorges in the red desert hills. Here they found villages huddled under the cliffs, and high on the cliff-faces, accessible only by wooden ladders, there were man-made caverns cut deep into the rock. Within them there were corridors and rooms, and in the old days of tribal war it was here that the villagers had stored the grain, and it was here that they had taken refuge in times of siege. Near the village of Zaouia Asaka they found caves which were still in use. The caverns of Asaka had more than a hundred and fifty chambers. Each family in the village owned one of these chambers, in which they stored their surplus grain. The sacks of corn were brought in by lowering them on ropes from the cliff top to people in the cave, who would catch the sacks with the aid of long hooks.

No one could tell when the caverns had been built, and it is quite possible that they were cut out of the rock by the Stone Age inhabitants of the Ounila valley. At first, perhaps, they were homes as well as store-houses. Certainly there has been a long tradition in Morocco that its original inhabitants were a race of cave-dwellers. In later ages, when agriculture improved, and times became more peaceful, villages were built in the valleys, and the caves were used only for storage.

Scattered along the Ounila there were several *zaouias*, housing the descendants of various saints. Their prosperity depended upon the reputation of their own particular *marabout*, for *zaouias* receive a considerable part of their livelihood from the gifts of suppliants. Humphrey and Colin found one *zaouia* whose ancestral *marabout* cannot have been over-endowed with *baraka*, for the village was now reduced to three men, two of them extremely old, living in a few pitiful ruins under an overhanging rock. Other *zaouias*, like Asaka, were prosperous, and boasted rows of neat houses, each with its shuttered windows.

At one place the travellers found a dead camel lying by the side of the track. Colin's zoological instincts were not to be denied, and although he had only a penknife he decided to disember the creature. The camel had been dead for some days, but Colin did not flinch from the grisly task. After some hours' work he had separated the skull and the bones of one leg. He loaded them on the mule, and continued the journey to Telouet.

CHAPTER ELEVEN

'Tartarin' Moves Again

Eppur si muove.
ATTRIBUTED TO GALILEO

Two days later John rejoined the party in Marrakesh. He and Thesiger had succeeded in climbing Djebel Toubkal, the 13,600 feet peak which is the highest mountain in the Atlas. On their journey they had collected many interesting specimens, including the flowers and seeds of a species of carnation that had hitherto been known only from a single dried specimen in the Museum at Rabat. They had also discovered a number of tree-frogs—in an alpine meadow at 12,000 feet! John found snails at a similar altitude. For a long time I was under the impression that these were the highest snails ever collected in Africa, but I have since discovered that there are more intrepid molluscs (and malacologists) in Tanganyika.

From Marrakesh we drove back over the dry plains to Beni Mellal, and beyond it to the village which was M'Barek's home. He very kindly offered to put us up for the night, and in the evening we met his stepfather, who was *taleb* of the settlement, and who had been imprisoned by the French because of his Nationalist sympathies. During the conversation Peter caused us acute discomfort by praising a sheepskin rug which he had noticed spread in one corner of the room.

'What a splendid rug,' he said. 'I wish they were still made like that in England.'

He continued inexorably to admire it. We were consumed with embarrassment, but our hushings and shushings were of no avail, and eventually M'Barek's stepfather, out of politeness, was obliged to give the rug to Peter. We felt very badly about this, and were uncertain how to repay him politely. It was a difficult situation, and M'Barek could not be called upon for advice. But we need not have worried, for on the following morning, just before we left, the *taleb* came out to the truck, noticed our paraffin pressure lamp, and admired it.

'What a splendid lamp,' he said. 'I wish we had lamps like that in Morocco.'

We departed lampless.

We were sorry to leave M'Barek, for in addition to his being a highly efficient interpreter, we had come to regard him as a friend. We realized how lucky we were to have found him. Someone else might have been equally good at translating, but could never have been such a cheerful and pleasant companion.

It was a sad farewell as the truck rumbled away down the dusty track between banks of prickly pears. M'Barek and his stepfather stood at their door waving, till finally we disappeared from their sight.

'Tartarin' rolled on through Beni Mellal, through Kasba Tadla and Oued Zem. In the last town we could see gutted buildings—sad reminders of the massacre of the twentieth. We spent a night in Rabat, camped on the lawn of the British Consulate-General, setting off for home on the following day. Soon we would be back in Oxford, back to the old routine of lectures and tutorials, of coffee-parties and interminable conversations—or so we thought.

We were coming into Souk-el-Arba, the last town before the border. It was a place where we had broken down before, and I was wondering if 'Tartarin' would make it this time when the engine spluttered, coughed and died. We coasted to a halt by the roadside, and Peter climbed underneath to unscrew the sump. When he had done so, practically the whole engine fell out—in a tangle of broken cylinders and twisted connecting-rods; several big-ends had gone simultaneously. It was damage that would take many days to repair, and a deep gloom settled over the party as we waited for a truck to tow us into the town.

In Souk-el-Arba we found a garage-proprietor who was willing to provide us with tools so that we could do our own repairs. We lived in his garage, setting up our beds and cooking our meals among the pools of oil that collected on the floor.

Our work on the truck did indeed take a long time. We were forced to dismantle the engine completely, and there was some doubt whether it would ever run again. Peter was obliged to make a journey to Casablanca in order to search for spares. I decided to go to Rabat: I would get more money from the Consulate and book passages by sea—just in case.

Rabat seemed much the same as before, still undisturbed by the country's internal conflicts, but I soon discovered that this was only a superficial impression. The discovery was very nearly fatal.

During my stay in the town I was accustomed to eat at an inexpensive French café, the *Gerbe d'Or*, which lay near the edge of the *medina*. I was on my way there one evening at dinner-time, and was within thirty yards of it when a man ran out of the *medina*. He threw something towards the tables which stood in front of the café, and a second later there was a thunderous explosion—then silence. The café was the scene of terrible destruction: tables were overturned, several people were lying grotesquely upon the ground, the glass front of the café was shattered. A crowd began to gather, police arrived, and, later, ambulances. There was no trace of the man who had thrown the bomb—he had merely run back into the *medina*. I ate dinner elsewhere.

Two days later I was back in Souk-el-Arba, for the repairs were progressing well and we had high hopes that the truck would soon be once more on the road. But there was still plenty of work to be done, and we spent a back-breaking day regrinding the valves and decarbonizing the cylinders.

In the afternoon two officers of the French Foreign Legion appeared with their jeep at the garage. While it was being repaired we chatted with them, and they invited us to join them for an evening's entertainment. Several of us accepted, and later in the evening the officers arrived in their car to pick us up. We visited some of the bars in Souk-el-Arba, and the party had become merry when one of our companions said: 'Now we must go to the club.' They drove us a short distance beyond the town to a small building from which issued sounds of music and laughter. We entered a large smoky room. Along one wall there was a bar, and on the opposite one a number of curtained cubicles. Tables were arranged across the intervening floor, and there were crowds of Legionaries with their companions. It might have been any slightly sordid night spot, but for one remarkable fact—all the women were absolutely naked. Our friends bought drinks, and we sat at one of the tables. Several rather unattractive girls appeared, and each one selected a victim to whom she devoted her attentions. In no time at all we were sitting in a circle, each one of us looking faintly surprised, with an undressed girl upon his knee. The Legionaries soon retired into the cubicles.

George Bernard Shaw has observed that, 'The Englishman thinks he

is moral when he is only uncomfortable.' We were certainly uncomfortable.

One member of our party had been working very hard all day, and
the heat and the drinks had become too much for him. He fell asleep in
his chair with the naked girl sitting on his knee, ineffectually stroking
his chin. He was completely oblivious of her attentions.

The ladies of the establishment were none too pleased that we failed
to make use of their services, but they were mollified when they discovered that we were English. That, it seemed, explained everything.
Are not the English, after all, the coldest race on earth?

*   *   *   *

While we were in Souk-el-Arba we met many French farmers from
the region. They were unanimous in their suspicion of the Moors, unanimous in their belief that the only solution to the Moroccan problem
was to have more soldiers and better police. There had been many acts
of terrorism in the region, mainly involving the burning of crops, and
the farmers had organized themselves into a private corps of vigilantes
to hunt down the incendiaries. The Moors were regularly searched for
concealed arms and ammunition. The French must have realized that
every time they publicly searched an Arab they were making themselves an enemy for life. To a Moroccan this was the greatest possible
affront to a man's dignity.

The fears of the Europeans were strengthened by events along the
northern border, for dissident Berber tribesmen from the mountains of
the Rif had descended across the border from Spanish Morocco, and
had pillaged several European settlements. A full-scale battle was going
on and the conflict was drawing nearer and nearer to Souk-el-Arba.
We were wondering whether we would get the truck repaired before
it reached the town. But in fact we did so, and, ten days late, we
crossed the border.

*   *   *   *

By now the Oxford term had started, and we ought already to have
been back at work. We determined, 'Tartarin' willing, to break all
records from Gibraltar to London. In Gibraltar we spent the night
once more on the eastern beach. It was damp, and the top of the Rock
was covered in mist. At three o'clock in the morning a policeman came
to tell us that it was dangerous to sleep there, because on nights such as

this pieces of rock break away and come thundering down on the beach. But so many people had told us—in so many different places—'it is unsafe to sleep here', that we scorned his advice. A few moments later we heard a faint sound at the top of the Rock, then a series of bangs, increasing in loudness till, with a 'grunt', a large stone landed on the gravel. We retreated behind the protective cover of the truck.

From Gibraltar we drove night and day, taking turns at the wheel; through Seville and Jerez, Madrid and Vittoria, back across the frontier into France at Hendaye. 'Tartarin' was going well. We did a thousand miles in two days. Then, bowling through France, the engine stopped. Fearfully we opened up the sump, but this time only one big-end had gone. We repaired it by the roadside in half a day—an achievement of which we were very proud. Then we rolled on, getting to the ferry at Dunkirk with only half an hour to spare.

We were received into the welcoming arms of the British Customs at Dover just two weeks late. We had done the journey from Gibraltar to England in three days.

We expected difficulties with the Customs explaining the contents of our boxes of specimens; the Moroccan pottery, the plants, the insects—and, of course, 'Herbert'. We determined to take precautions. The head of the camel which Colin had dismembered by the banks of the Ounila had been sitting on the roof of the truck. By now its smell was absolutely beyond description, and before we left the ferry at Dover we transferred it into the back. Then we carefully laced up the canvas cover.

The Customs officer bristled with efficiency.

'Where have you come from?' he asked.

'Morocco.'

'Hmmm. Better have a look in the back, please.'

He untied the lacing, and pulled open the canvas. A great wave of decaying camel engulfed him. He staggered back, and, two shades paler, groped his way round to the front of the truck.

'I think we will consider the examination as made,' he said.

We drove joyfully into the green countryside of Kent.

The truck never got to Oxford. It broke down finally in Haywards Heath, and we were obliged to take the train. Nobody noticed our triumphal return to the City—but then, nobody had noticed our departure.

Epilogue

'OXFORD EXPLORERS MISSING.' The headline appeared in one of the undergraduate newspapers on the day of our return. Some enterprising amateur newsman had discovered that we were overdue, and in true journalistic tradition had jumped to his own conclusions. We had, he hinted, probably been massacred by the terrorists. The article was inaccurate, but entertaining to read—in much the same way, I should imagine, as one's own obituary in *The Times*.

Oxford had not changed during our absence, but it is difficult to believe that Oxford ever changes. I found it an amusing mental exercise to try to visualize it as did the men of Idirh, as an oasis in the desert of southern England; to picture a caravan of supercilious camels plodding carefully through the dust of High Street, past the palm-girt colleges, to wind slowly up the rocky mule-track to the top of Shotover Hill. In the evening, perhaps, one would hear the *muezzin* calling from the top of Magdalen Tower, and the Heads of Colleges would be prostrating themselves upon their lawns. There would be French soldiers patrolling the streets or breaking up a demonstration of undergraduates who shouted, 'England for the English. End the Protectorate.'

The demonstrators would be encouraged by the wild cries of veiled undergraduettes who sat apart on the roof of the examination schools. . . .

* * * *

We gradually sank back into the routine of university life, and it became more and more difficult for us to realize that we had travelled seven thousand miles since the previous term. Recollection was difficult even in spite of the multitudinous jobs that had to be done.

The business of an expedition does not end when it reaches home. Indeed, before then it has hardly begun. There are letters to be written, supplies to be disposed of, specimens to be catalogued, accounts to be drawn up.

'Dear Humphrey,

Could you give me some idea of how you spent the five thousand francs I gave you at Tamdaght? . . .'

'Dear John,

I hope you have managed to get rid of the canvas bath. . . .'

The work continued, and from time to time one paused to wonder whether it was all worth it. Looking back, I asked myself what we had achieved. Certainly, we had collected new species of animals and plants; Charles Pasternak had found a blood abnormality new to Morocco; the glazes used in the pottery at Zerekten were apparently of great interest; we had perhaps added a little to knowledge of Berber life. Nevertheless, these seemed to be meagre results for the effort and expenditure which went into the enterprise.

Yet, to me at any rate, the effort was justified for another reason. We had learned a good deal from meeting people and situations that we would otherwise have missed. We had all grown a little wiser—not much, but a little.

* * * *

Since our return, events in Morocco have changed the country's whole political structure. Sultan Sidi Mohammed V has returned from exile. El-Glaoui, the old Pasha of Marrakesh, is dead—and before his death he prostrated himself before the man he had helped to expel. The French have left Morocco; it is no longer a Protectorate, but an independent nation. Yet many French settlers and officials remain, and one can only hope that the Moroccans will remember with gratitude the good that the French have done in their country, and that they will forget with magnanimity the evil.

It is rumoured that the tribes in the mountains and in the south have returned to their old lawless ways, that many independent 'armies of liberation' roam the Sahara, fighting and pillaging, that there have been uprisings in the Atlas against the Sultan. But I do not know the truth of these stories, nor have I heard any news of the Ait Rbaa in particular. Perhaps the old men of the villages no longer have cause for nostalgia about the good old days of tribal war.

It may be that I shall never be able to return to the valley, yet it has become part of me, and I have an irrational half-belief that events in Idirh and the fortunes of its inhabitants will affect me even over the miles that separate us. I shall remember them for a long time, and no doubt they will remember us. Our visit must have been sufficiently unusual to stay in their minds, and we have left our marks behind us. Who knows that a future anthropologist will not be surprised to find a Berber tribe in which widespread use is made of polythene bags, in which water is served to the passing traveller from a tin marked 'Simpson's Ready Dinners', in which Englishmen have a reputation— for their inability to shoot?

'Tartarin' has been sold and has gone on another journey. It has been repainted, its name has been changed, and different people have sat and slept and squabbled in it. Its character is no longer the same. I understand that it is even in good mechanical condition.

Some time after our return to Oxford I went to a cocktail party and there I met an acquaintance.

'Hullo,' he said. 'Haven't seen you for many a year. Hear you've been in foreign parts—Algeria wasn't it? Hope you didn't have too much trouble with the wogs.'

I wanted to tell him about the 'wogs' who had stood guard over us in the Palmeries at Marrakesh, about Lhassan and Mohammed-one-mule, about the men who entertained us so hospitably in their homes. But it was no use.

'No,' I said lamely, 'we didn't have too much trouble.'

Oxford University Expedition to Southern Morocco, 1955

Members of the party were:

B. C. Clarke (Magdalen), Zoologist, Leader.

T. H. Beckett (Worcester), Ethnologist.

P. Galloway (Merton), Geographer.

J. G. B. Newbould (Merton), Botanist.

C. J. Pennycuick (Merton), Zoologist.

We were joined in the field by:

C. Pasternak (Magdalen), Biochemist.

Mouhsine M'Barek (Berber College, Azrou), Interpreter.

SCIENTIFIC RESULTS

(1) *Geographical*

The original intention was to complete a land-use survey of two separate areas, one on the northern, and other on the southern, slope of the mountains. However, the first village selected for the survey (Idirh) presented such problems that the time we had allowed for field work was taken up on the northern slope alone.

Galloway drew a map (1:5,000) of the village and its surrounding agricultural land, and noted the distribution and rotation of crops. It proved difficult to persuade the villagers to disclose the *ownership* of fields, but eventually we managed to plot the extent of the holdings of one 'rich' and one 'poor' man. The pattern of Seguias (irrigation channels) was mapped and information on the system of water-rights was obtained.

Beckett made a study of the political and social organization of the six villages which comprise the *fraction* of the Ait Rbaa, and of their relation to the central power of the Glaoui family at Telouet. In addition, some comparison was made with communities on the southern slopes, which are also under the authority of Telouet.

We took notes on native crafts including housebuilding, weaving, construction and use of agricultural implements, woodwork, iron-mongery, etc. Beckett made a collection of local pottery and other crafts for the Pitt-Rivers Museum. The potteries of the area had not been previously studied.

Beckett and Galloway studied transhumance, both in the mountains and in the desert.

(2) Anthropological

Pasternak, during his short stay, was able to investigate the distribution of abnormal haemoglobins, using a portable paper-electrophoresis apparatus. He did the bulk of his work in the hospital at Ouazazate and discovered the presence of blood abnormalities which had not been reported from this area (see Pasternak and Roberts, 'Man', 1956, 52).

(3) Botanical

Newbould collected about six hundred species of plants over a wide area, and brought back a number of roots and seeds to be grown in this country. He also made a preliminary investigation of the relation between water-content and water-deficit for a species of *Cystus*, and observed how this ratio differed with altitude, temperature and community type.

(4) Zoological

We concentrated our studies upon the Invertebrates, since there was a greater chance of discovering local races and relicts among the less mobile species. Pennycuick's walk considerably enlarged the scope of the work. Over 5,500 preserved specimens were brought back to this country, including:

4,500 Insects	15 Amphibians
250 Other Arthropods	40 Reptiles
400 Earthworms	2 Birds
500 Molluscs	4 Mammals

A live Barbary ground squirrel, *Atlantoxerus getulus*, was brought back and given to the Regent's Park Zoo.

Pennycuick and Clarke made a survey of the distribution of short-horned grasshoppers, attempting to relate their distribution to altitude and habitat-type.

(5) *Other Activities*

Newbould ascended a number of peaks, including Djebel Toubkal, Djebel Tistouit and Djebel Isirhs. There is no previous record of the ascent of the last two.

POINTS OF INTEREST TO FUTURE EXPEDITIONS

In general, we cannot overstress the importance of consulting national and local authorities on the aims and itinerary of an expedition, and of maintaining a close liaison with them.

Information about Morocco can be obtained from:

Organizations

Office Marocain de Tourisme, Rue Maurice-Pascoriet, Rabat.

Le Syndicat d'Initiative de Marrakesh, Rue Commandant Haring, Marrakesh.

Institut Scientifique Cherifien, Avenue Biarnay, Rabat (for Zoology, Botany, Geography, etc.).

Institut des Hautes-Etudes Marocaines, Avenue Biarnay, Rabat.

Books

The *Michelin Guide for Morocco* is invaluable.

G.-H. Bousquet, *L'Islam Maghrebin* (Maison de Livres, Algiers).

R. Landau, *Invitation to Morocco* (Faber & Faber).

E. Laoust, *Cours de Berbère Marocain, dialects du Sous, du Haut et de L'Anti-Atlas* (Challamel, Paris, 1946).

P. Mayne, *The Alleys of Marrakesh* (John Murray).

R. Montaigne, *Les Berbères et le Makhzen dans le Sud du Maroc* (Librairie Félix Alcan, Paris).

B. Newman, *Morocco To-day* (Robert Hale).

H. Terasse, *Histoire du Maroc* (Atlantides, Casablanca).

Maps

Michelin, Nos. 170 and 171.

Survey 1 in 100,000 produced by the Institut Géographique National, Rabat.

A few other points are worth noting:

(a) It is possible, given a strong digestion, to live off the land. However, we took a number of 'luxury' foods. Of these we would particularly recommend: tinned milk, tinned margarine, marmalade, and large quantities of boiled sweets.

(b) Details of travel to Morocco can be found in the *Michelin Guide*. In addition to the means mentioned therein it is possible to travel by sea direct from England. Many ships of the P. & O., Union Castle and British-Indian lines call at Tangier: so do those of Rotterdam Lloyd from Southampton. Cargo ships go direct to Casablanca.

Normally, the cost of overland travel to an expedition would be a little less than by ship, but because of two serious breakdowns it would have been £80 to £100 cheaper for the party to have gone by sea.

(c) It is advisable to employ labour (other than interpreters) through the local sheikh. Not only is this in accordance with local custom but he has greater disciplinary powers than any expedition would wish for.

(d) After the first week we employed a boy for carrying water from the spring, washing up, and so on. Stomach upsets immediately ensued, but much time was saved.

Apart from the internal disorders just mentioned, the health of the party was good. We had been vaccinated and given T.A.B. injections, and we all took a daily 'Paludrine' pill although malaria is not very common in the region. Good drinking water can usually be obtained from mountain springs, and we did not have to use the water filter.

(e) We recommend future expeditions to take a large supply of simple remedies, adequate to cure the more easily recognizable minor ailments, but unable to do harm when used as a placebo. There will be a heavy local demand for them. Where normal medical aid is not generally available even a placebo seems to have remarkable curative powers.

ACKNOWLEDGMENTS

It is a great pleasure to acknowledge our debt of gratitude to the many individuals and organizations whose gifts, advice and other help have made the expedition possible.

We would like to thank especially the senior members of the Exploration Club, and above all Dr K. S. Sandford, Mr R. W. Steel, and Dr J. M. Houston.

We are very grateful to the following for financial support:

Oxford University; The Alexander Allan Paton Memorial Fund; *The National Geographic Magazine*; The Royal Geographical Society;

The Geographical Magazine Trust Fund; the Spalding Trust; The Department of Zoology and Comparative Anatomy, Oxford; The Ashmolean Museum; The Grocers' Company; Merton College; All Souls College; The Oxford Botanic Garden; The A. C. Irvine Fund; Worcester College; The Hatters Society.

We are most grateful also to all those who helped us in Morocco, particularly to Mrs Dunlop of Tangier, who entertained us royally, to Mr Freese-Pennyfather and his staff at the Consulate-General in Rabat for innumerable kindnesses, and to Madame Racine and General Brissaud-Desmaillet for their most generous hospitality. For advice and help in many other ways we are much indebted to:

Madame Allouche le Page; Dr A. E. Allport; Miss B. Blackwood; The President of Magdalen; M. de la Boissière of the Contrôle Civil, Ait Ourir; Brigadier G. Bomford, O.B.E., the British Consul-General, Tangier; Mr A. D. H. Bivar; Dr A. J. Cain; Mr D. J. Chaundy; Dr C. A. Clarke; the Commandants and staff of the Bureaux des Affaires Indigènes, Tazenakht, Agdz and Zagora; Professor C. D. Darlington, F.R.S.; M. Denis, of the Contrôle Civil, Region de Marrakech; Miss S. Erlbeck: Air Commodore F. W. Felgate, C.B.E.; Brigadier B. E. Fergusson, C.B.E., D.S.O.; Mr G. G. Faudree; Mr and Mrs E. Gellner; Mr R. Gifford; M. Gilloteaux of the Service Générale de l'Information, Rabat; H. E. Si Abd. Cadek el-Glaoui; His Late Excellency Si Hadj Thami el-Glaoui, Pasha of Marrakesh; Professor A. C. Hardy, F.R.S.; M. Horlaville, of the Institut Géographique Nationale, Annexe du Maroc; Dr H. B. D. Kettlewell; The Khalifa of Telouet; The Director of the Royal Geographical Society; The Khalifa of Tamdaght; Mr J. La Gorce; The Provost of Worcester; Dr T. F. Mitchell; The Warden of Merton; Dr F. L. Patry; Dr J. B. Panouse of the Institut Scientifique Cherifien, Rabat; Dr H. W. Parker; Mr G. A. Potter; H. E. The Governor of Gibraltar; Dr D. F. Roberts; Mr N. D. Riley; Dr P. M. Sheppard; Mr G. G. Simpson; Marshal of the Royal Air Force Sir John C. Slessor, G.C.B., D.S.O., M.C.; The Warden of All Souls; Mr R. Sutton; Dr G. Taylor; Mr W. Thesiger, D.S.O.; Mr H. R. Trevor-Roper; Sir Douglas Veale; Dr F. Whitehead; Mr M. Williamson.

And for gifts of materials, equipment or services:

The Ac-Delco Division of General Motors Ltd; The Automatic Coil Winder and Electrical Equipment Ltd; Albright and Wilson Ltd; Biro-Swan Ltd; Thos. Black & Sons (Greenock) Ltd; B. H. Blackwell

Ltd; The Bland Line; Boots Pure Drug Co. Ltd; British Drug Houses Ltd; The British School of Motoring Ltd; British Visqueen Ltd; Bryant and May Ltd; B.S.A. (Guns) Ltd; Capurro's Central Garage Ltd, Gibraltar; Chance and Hunt; Chloride Batteries Ltd; C. and J. Clark Ltd; Frank Cooper Ltd; G. R. Cooper (Oxford) Ltd; Crosse and Blackwell Ltd; The Ever Ready Co. (Great Britain) Ltd; Ferrodo Ltd; The Ford Motor Co. Ltd; Glaxo Laboratories Ltd; B. J. Harris; Hunt and Broadhurst Ltd; Huntley and Palmer Ltd; Ilco Ltd; Imperial Chemical Industries Ltd; Johnson and Johnson (Great Britain) Ltd; Krafts Ltd; Laboratoires Avlon; Lincoln Cars Ltd; Lintafoam Industries Ltd; Joseph Lucas Ltd; Marmite Ltd; The Measham Motor Sales Organization; National Pressure Cookers; Nestles Ltd; Panette Holloware Ltd; Polarizers (United Kingdom) Ltd; Pyrene Ltd; Quaker Oats Ltd; Roche Products Ltd; Rolls Razor Co.; Simpsons Ready Foods Ltd; T. J. Smith and Nephew Ltd; Smith's English Clocks Ltd; Tate and Lyle Ltd; Tewel Industries Ltd; Van den Berghs Ltd; C. C. Wakefield Ltd; Wilkinson Sword Co. Ltd; Williams and Williams Ltd.

ACCOUNTS

Income	£	s.	d.
Oxford University	20	0	0
Members' contributions	400	0	0
Alexander Allan Paton Memorial Fund	141	0	0
National Geographic Magazine	100	0	0
Royal Geographical Society	50	0	0
Geographical Magazine Trust Fund	50	0	0
H.N. Spalding Trust	50	0	0
Department of Zoology, Oxford	50	0	0
Grocers' Company	25	0	0
Merton College	25	0	0
All Souls College	15	0	0
Botanic Gardens, Oxford	10	0	0
A.C. Irvine Fund	10	0	0
Worcester College	5	0	0
Ashmolean Museum	5	0	0
Hatters Society	4	3	0
From Insurances	12	14	0
Publications	90	3	8
Other Income	15	0	0
Total Income £1,088		0	8

Expenditure	£	s.	d.	£	s.	d.
EQUIPMENT						
Camping and General	199	18	8			
Scientific	11	12	2			
Maps	3	10	0			
Stationery, etc.	14	2	11			
Total	229	3	9			
Less Sale	115	0	0			
Net Equipment	114	3	9	114	3	9
FOOD						
Total Food	37	9	3			
Less Sale	21	6	8			
Net Food	16	2	7	16	2	7
PHOTOGRAPHIC						
Film	27	2	11			
Camera	32	17	1			
Processing	13	19	5			
Total Photographic	73	19	5			
Less Sale of Camera	24	0	0			
Net Photographic	49	19	5	49	19	5
INSURANCE						
Equipment	12	0	0			
Life and Injury at £12 each	60	0	0			
Total Insurance	72	0	0	72	0	0
FORMALITIES						
Visas	14	13	4			
Customs (Oxford)	2	12	6			
Customs Dunkirk	6	18	3			
Bank Charges	16	17	8			
Total Formalities	40	11	9	40	11	9
ORGANIZATION						
Telephone, Postage, Personal Visits, Clerical and sundries	30	3	6	30	3	6
TRANSPORT						
(i) *Vehicle*						
Cost	55	0	0			
Reconditioning	163	3	11			
Spares	26	15	0			
Licences, Insurance, etc.	42	13	5			
Total Vehicle	287	12	4			
Less Sale	150	0	0			
Net Vehicle	137	12	4			
(ii) *Running Expenses*						
Petrol (7,000 miles at an average ten m.p.g. and an average cost of 3s. 8d. gallon)	131	0	0			
Ferry Dover-Dunkirk return	63	2	6			
Ferry Gibraltar-Tangier return	21	10	0			
Food and lodging on journey (at 5s. 9d. per man-day)	63	0	0			

	£	s.	d.	£	s.	d.
Hotel Expenses Taddert (8 men for a week)	27	0	0			
Repairs	68	11	0			
Expedition contribution to Beckett's return fare	8	0	0			
Total Running Expenses	382	4	4			
Total Transport				519	16	8

FIELD EXPENSES

	£	s.	d.	£	s.	d.
Food (at 2s. 6d. per man-day)	49	17	0			
Transport						
Mules	8	4	0			
Petrol and bus fares	2	14	0			
Total Transport	10	18	0			
Local Labour						
Interpreter (£5 per week)	45	0	0			
Servant (£2 2s. per week)	12	12	0			
Casual labour	4	19	0			
Total Labour	62	11	0			
Payment for Specimens	10	13	0			
Total for Subsidiary Expeditions	72	13	0			
Sundries	6	5	0			
Total Field Expenses				212	17	0
Expedition Contribution to O.U. Exploration Club Bulletin				10	0	0
Further Expenditure				22	6	0
TOTAL EXPENDITURE				£1,088	0	8